**GREAT MINDS.
GREAT WEALTH.
GREAT FOR
YOUR 401K.**

# GREAT MINDS.
# GREAT WEALTH.
# GREAT FOR
# YOUR 401K.

## HOW TO RAISE YOUR RETURN, REDUCE YOUR RISK AND CUT YOUR COST

RODNEY SCHULZ

 iUniverse®

**GREAT MINDS. GREAT WEALTH.**
**GREAT FOR YOUR 401K.**
**HOW TO RAISE YOUR RETURN, REDUCE**
**YOUR RISK AND CUT YOUR COST**

*iUniverse books may be ordered through booksellers or by contacting:*

*iUniverse*
*1663 Liberty Drive*
*Bloomington, IN 47403*
*www.iuniverse.com*
*1-800-Authors (1-800-288-4677)*

*ISBN: 978-1-5320-6946-8 (sc)*
*ISBN: 978-1-5320-6944-4 (hc)*
*ISBN: 978-1-5320-6945-1 (e)*

*Print information available on the last page.*

*iUniverse rev. date: 03/16/2020*

# CONTENTS

# INTRODUCTION

Whether you're a novice investor with a small portfolio or a seasoned investor sitting on millions of dollars, you're likely inundated with financial opinions. Unfortunately, when it comes to our personal wealth we're all vulnerable to emotions. Therefore, most "financial" writers target emotions instead of explaining the facts in a way that is fun and interesting to read.

Nevertheless, there is hope and the cure is painless. In short, this book:

A. Presents an easy-to-understand, non-commercial, sound, concise body of pragmatic investment knowledge to help you; and

B. Does this in a way that is highly informative for the seasoned investor while not overwhelming to the novice investor.

Putting this information to work will allow you to:

1) Raise your return to ultimately ***make you wealthier.***

2)  Reduce your risk *to immediately decrease your investment heartburn.*

3)  Cut your cost so that *you have more money to spend on the fun things of life.*

An Added Bonus. Wouldn't you rather spend more time on the golf course, relaxing on the beach or enjoying your children and grandchildren? Enabling you to do this is another objective of this book, as most individuals have better things to do with their time than read and study mounds of information that has little or no value to their personal wealth. In fact, most investment "news and information," if acted on, hurts, rather than helps, the investor. As you can see, this is a real win for you and those around you.

## My Unique Position to Help You

Smart and well-educated finance professionals are a dime a dozen. They're everywhere, and investment books are ubiquitous.

The thing that makes this book different is my ability to decipher what really matters and put pragmatic Nobel Prize level financial knowledge in common terms for your application and benefit. This information will get you the maximum return for the amount of risk and cost. Moreover, it will help you understand and assess your risk while knowing the likely limits of your portfolio.

My Early Years. Unlike 99 percent of all top-tier MBAs (I got my MBA through the full time, day time program at Duke University's Fuqua School of Business), I grew up in a family where neither parent attended any college. My father was a blue-collar oil field worker and my mother drove a school bus. I honestly don't know if any of my grandparents even graduated from high school. My father's father was a life-long farmer in central Kansas, while my mother's father spent his working life as a blue-collar worker in the oil fields of northeast Oklahoma and central Kansas.

No, my parents definitely weren't stupid. However, I can still remember many typical family dinner conversations where Dad ranted about his frustration with "engineers who don't have any common sense" and my mother always being uneasy around people "with money."

Nevertheless, I must have inherited some degree of cerebral capacity from them, as an engineering ability test I took in high school put my mechanical aptitude in the top 1 percent and my ACT math score was in the top 2 percent. Ten years later I scored a perfect 35/35 on the Analysis of Business Situations section of the Graduate Management Admissions Test (GMAT) and my combined math and English skills were in the top 4 percent of all college graduates. But again, and I truly mean this, smart and well-educated finance professionals are a dime a dozen.

After paying 100 percent of my way through a petroleum engineering degree at the University of Kansas I soon, like just about all engineers, found myself surrounded by other smart and well-educated people. As a young petroleum engineer I often worked on things as abstract as oil, gas and water flowing through the pores of rock thousands of feet underground. Another problem I worked on was to calculate the amount thousands of feet of steel pipe would stretch (due to weight, heat and external pressure) and shrink (due to internal pressure) when put in operation. I ran computer simulations on the above challenges, as well as many other situations. Things could get complicated quickly.

However, my ultimate job as a petroleum engineer was really quite simple:

1) How many dollars went into the hole?
2) What were the associated risks?
3) How many dollars would we likely get out of the hole?

This is very simple and very much like your financial situation; i.e.,

1) How many dollars should go into various segments of your portfolio?
2) What are the risks of each segment?
3) How much can you reasonably expect to get out of your portfolio over an unknown period of time?

In answering the three questions above concerning oil and gas situations countless times in just a few years, I realized there must be more to financial management than what I learned in one three-credit engineering economics course. Thus, I chose to invest much of what I had saved in five years of petroleum engineering work to finance an MBA from Duke University's Fuqua School of Business through their full-time, day-time program.

## An Abrupt Turn of Events

A few years after graduating from Duke my wife and I moved to Pittsburgh, PA, her hometown, for a variety of personal reasons. Not long thereafter, I found myself interviewing for the position of Financial Director/chief financial officer (CFO) for a 25-year-old college campus ministry organization with 150 employees in six states. Although it was a "non-profit" organization, we had a multi-million-dollar budget for operating expenses and a multi-million-dollar endowment fund invested in stocks and bonds.

To be sure, I really didn't want the position when I first interviewed for it. In fact, I went in to the interview hoping they would find someone else. But they made it clear: They wanted me. Their finance department was a mess (much more-so than they disclosed or anyone realized), and I had a track record of fixing things with an eye toward good financial management.

Again, this was NOT a position I initially wanted. Working in the shadow (literally) of a housing project high-rise apartment building in Pittsburgh's second roughest neighborhood was not what I had in mind when I left a major oil company to pay my way through Duke. Having an office in the shadow of a housing project is not what top-tier MBAs aspire to do. Working 55 to 65 hours a week for $25,000 per year (approximately $8.50 per hour) was not what I had planned, especially when the agreement was for 35 hours a week. But it was in my Maker's cards, and His purposes trump my purposes. Thus, the work began.

## How this Experience Applies to You

After starting at the campus ministry organization I soon realized the key challenge. No, it wasn't having a $4 million "balance sheet" that was $98,000 out of balance. No, it wasn't the ten IRS fines levied on the organization in the five years before my arrival. And no, it wasn't a long list of other problems of similar alarm level and urgency.

What was the key challenge? No one understood anything about finance or accounting. And as long as they got their paycheck on time, they really didn't care.

Our employees had a wide range of interests and talents that included playing the guitar, sharing their faith, leading outdoor wilderness experiences and making people laugh. However, most of them were mathematically challenged and really didn't care, as long as they had enough money to pay the rent in a low-cost apartment and buy enough food to survive. This is good, as it's what college campus ministers are generally made of.

Nevertheless, nothing happened without money moving and I often found myself having to explain why various things were necessary to run the organization's finances in a way that were prudent, responsible and efficient. Hence, in communicating I had to be simple, relevant and concise. I had to boil my every move down to why it mattered to the individual I was dealing with.

*That's just like this book: I'll make it simple, relevant and concise*, boiling it all down to what matters to you, why it matters and what you can do about the situation to raise your return, reduce your risk and cut your cost. This will enhance your personal finances so that you get a bigger paycheck with less heartburn when it comes to living on your portfolio during retirement.

The Board Members and Meetings. In addition to dealing with the campus ministers and their supervisors on a daily basis, I also made the quarterly financial presentation to the Board of Directors. This presented an even more challenging situation than dealing with the campus ministers.

Why? Because our board members included an engineer who was the former vice chairman of Chevron, a CPA who was the former president of General Nutrition Center (GNC, the nationwide health food and vitamin retailer) and a CPA who was also the CFO of a major hospital. However, at the same time, the board included some very influential and affluent homemakers, including the wife of the president of U.S. Steel, the largest steel company in the United States, and the widow of a former chief executive officer (CEO) of Consolidated Coal Company, the largest coal company in the United States. And then, for good measure, the board included a couple of academics, two ministers and the director of pediatric neurosurgery at Children's Hospital of Pittsburgh. That's a diverse and challenging group.

*My job? In a matter of minutes, I had to lay out the finances in a way that was easy to understand for the non-financial types while also not insulting or boring the corporate executives.* The questions ranged from very simple to insightful, difficult and complex. But every question was important, as it was coming from a high-value supporter or a minister they all admired. And I had to accomplish it all in five to seven minutes, as everyone was attending the meeting on lunch break.

The better I did my job, the easier it was for the organization's president and CEO to raise money from the board members.

Whether the donor was a homemaker or an executive, they would open their checkbooks more liberally if they were confident of my financial acumen and the organization's overall efficiency.

Excluding the objective of raising money, the quarterly board meetings were similar to the objective of this book: ***To communicate the truly relevant information in a way that speaks to the most sophisticated investors while not overwhelming the novice investor.*** Just like I had to do at the board meetings, in this book I have to make everything count while keeping it brief and interesting.

The Investment Committee Meetings. As well as making the quarterly financial report to the Board and communicating to the ministry staff while running the daily financial operations, I also had a key part serving the organization's endowment fund investment committee.

The endowment fund had millions of dollars invested in stocks and bonds through the area's largest regional bank. Of course, the committee included the most seasoned executives on our board of directors. These executives were on many other boards and endowment fund investment committees. Additionally, the founder and CEO of the regional bank was one of our directors. Hence, we had access to some of the bank's best portfolio's managers. Why? The managers and executives between the portfolio and the bank CEO wanted to make sure the endowment fund did well, as they knew the results would soon make it to the top of their organization. And, moreover, the results of the endowment fund investments would soon be communicated to other wealthy and highly influential citizens of Pittsburgh and reflect accordingly on the bank's founder and CEO.

I immediately realized the education I was receiving through serving in the position. I also realized, once again, the challenge of the situation. What was it? I had to take the complicated investment jargon the executives spoke during the meeting and immediately put it into short, easy to understand terms for the campus ministry organization's CEO, a minister. He, in turn, would communicate the information to both homemakers and sophisticated executives in his efforts to raise more money for the endowment fund.

For a number of reasons beyond the scope of this book, one being the diagnosis and treatment of my Tourette's syndrome, I chose to resign my position at the campus ministry organization after serving in the position a little under three years. Although my time at the organization was short, the experience was invaluable on a number of fronts, especially in shaping my views on investment finance.

## Going Back into the Oil and Gas Industry.

Where did I go upon leaving the campus ministry organization? Back to a major oil company as the financial point person and leadership team member for the largest contiguous oil and gas lease in the Gulf of Mexico (52 platforms with hundreds of wells and the supporting infrastructure).

While at the major oil company it took almost no time before my boss and others started asking me how they should invest their personal 401(k) plan holdings. They realized from informal conversations that I truly understood investment finance and portfolio management. Others also realized I could get to the heart of the matter very quick and put things in very simple terms.

Ironically, several months after relocating from Pittsburgh to Lafayette, LA, my new neurologist changed the medication for Tourette's syndrome to one with minimal side effects, a medication I'm still taking daily, 19+ years later. If this would have happened while I lived in Pittsburgh, I would likely still be there. However, it wasn't meant to be.

Soon after returning to the major oil company, oil prices plunged to $13 per barrel and I was transferred to the company's Houston lubricants office. Once again, it didn't take long for fellow employees to start asking me questions about investment finance and portfolio management.

## Moving into Personal Financial Management

After I had served in three successively higher responsibility roles in three years, the company merged with another oil company and those I had hoped would help move my career forward left the organization. However, because my wife and I were in the midst of two international adoptions that took a total of five years, I didn't want to upset the employment situation. So what did I do? I kept my daytime position with the major oil company while changing my career focus to part-time financial advisory work.

From the beginning I knew my target audience would be clients with an engineering and/or financial background, as they would appreciate my highly analytical background and approach to the situation. *And from my first client forward, I learned that I needed to frequently draw on my experience at communicating complicated information in simple terms quickly and simultaneously to both technical and non-technical types.*

Why? I usually dealt with married couples in which one had a technical/analytical skillset while the other didn't. I knew that if the non-technical spouse didn't understand and wasn't comfortable with my recommendations, he/she wouldn't be long for my financial advisory services. The couple always knew their relationship was far more important than my financial advice. They could hire and fire financial advisors on a whim, but they were committed to each other for life. Thus, I had to communicate the information effectively to both of them.

My challenge there was like my challenge with this book: I had to put things in simple, non-abstract terms that everyone would understand and appreciate while not boring anyone. Just as I do in this book, I took pragmatic, proven Nobel Prize level information and put it in simple terms that everyone can understand while stretching the minds of the financially astute.

In the words and observation of one of my clients, I have "the heart of a teacher rather than the heart of a salesman." The result?

My clients all successfully weathered the financial crisis of 2008. Moreover, I have a more than 95-percent annual client retention ratio. Why? I believe it's because my clients understand the foundation of what I teach them and what I apply, the same things I communicate in this book: strategies and tactics that are fundamentally sound and deliver strong results.

Again, the objective is to:

- Raise your return
- Reduce your risk
- Cut your cost

This is what I'm about. It's always a joy and a privilege to see investors eyes light up at seeing the simplicity and logic behind what I communicate, while doing it in minimal time. Thank you for your time, consideration and interest. I believe you'll enjoy the journey ahead, through this book and beyond.

NOTE: Because this book was written over a period of twelve years and to provide a broad base of information, the time frames for data and examples vary.

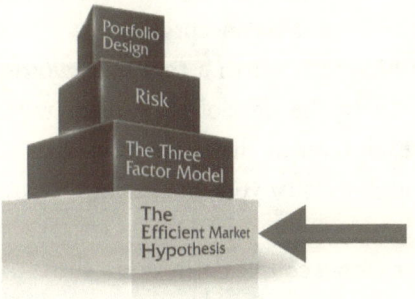

# CHAPTER 1

# The Efficient Market

> **Unconventional Wisdom**
> *The market does a better job of picking stocks than an Ivy League stock analyst wearing a $2000 suit. Moreover, it does so with less risk and at a fraction of the cost. How? Read on, as it's surprisingly common-sensical....*

If you are reading this book, you probably want to:

- *Raise your return*
- *Reduce your risk*
- *Cut your cost*

Helping you chart a course to accomplish the above is the essence of this book. Fortunately, it's not a long or difficult process. In fact, to the chagrin of all the professional stock pickers and portfolio managers of the world, it's rather easy. Moreover, you won't need to absorb a lexicon of investment jargon to master the basics. Instead, it's a matter of a few simple concepts.

Because "a picture is worth a thousand words," we're going to build the pyramid at the start of each chapter. Step by step, we'll work through each layer of the pyramid so that you'll understand things well enough to trust your life savings to what you'll learn in this short book.

Let me start with a couple definitions. First, the most common types of securities (investments) are stocks and bonds. Stock is actually part ownership of a corporation. In other words, if you own shares in McDonald's, for example, you could be said to be a part owner or have "equity" in McDonald's. This is why stocks are also called equities.

A second type of investment (security) is a bond, which is just a loan to the company or government. These loans can be short term loans, such as CDs and U.S. Treasury Bills, which commonly come due (mature) in under 36 months. Longer term loans are commonly referred to as "bonds". In short, all loans are bonds.

A *mutual fund* is an investment, or security, that is comprised of other securities, such as stocks and bonds. Mutual funds can have dozens, or even thousands, of securities.

An *equity mutual fund* is comprised of stocks, while a *bond mutual fund* or *fixed income fund* is comprised of bonds. Of course, many, if not most, mutual funds contain both stocks and bonds.

In short, a mutual fund is a pool of money supplied by investors who pay a person or entity to manage it for them. A key thought behind mutual funds is that a professional hired to manage everyone's money can generate a better return than individual investors. Another benefit of mutual funds is that the cost is spread over many investors.

Many people are suspicious of mutual funds or believe they can do better picking stocks and bonds on their own. However, that practice is little different from the mutual fund model because an individual is still picking what to buy and sell.

As you can see, the base layer of the pyramid is something called the efficient market hypothesis. A hypothesis is a reasonable explanation. This hypothesis states that a free and open market, such as the New York Stock Exchange (NYSE), has two key characteristics:

1. It incorporates all available information almost instantaneously.
2. Security price movements follow a random-walk model[1,2].

The above points may sound innocent, unimposing and uninspiring, but they are easy to apply in ways that will significantly increase your wealth. Why? These principles affect every market you see, ranging from a bottle of ketchup to the house or apartment you live in to the price of a jumbo jet. And the above two principles speak to every asset in your investment portfolio.

Before diving further into the efficient market hypothesis, we first need to ask "what is a random walk?" Fortunately, the answer is easy.

Before going into any graphs, etc., think about children playing a game in which they blindfold someone, spin them around 20 times and ask them to walk to the best of their ability–while blindfolded –forward or backward or to either side. What does this create? A random walk.

Taking this analogy to the investment arena, you now understand how randomly security prices move. To illustrate this we can look at the percent price change of the S&P 500 from random time periods (Figures 1.1 and 1.2). From these you can see the random walk of security prices, and this randomness will exist over any time period chosen.

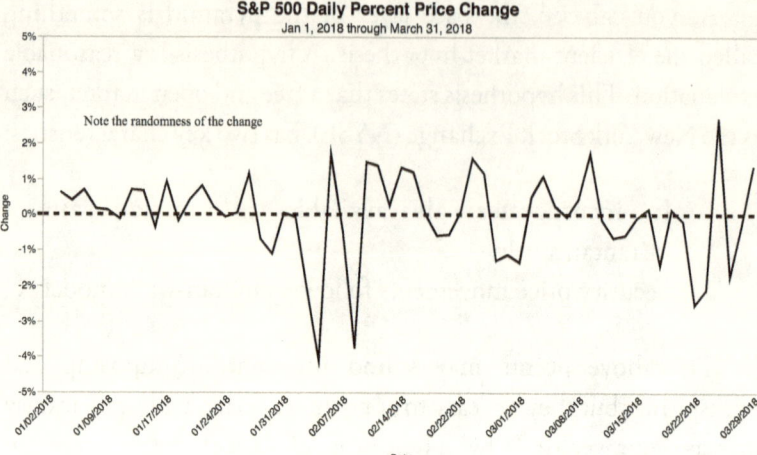

**Figure 1.1**
**Daily Random Walk of the S&P 500**

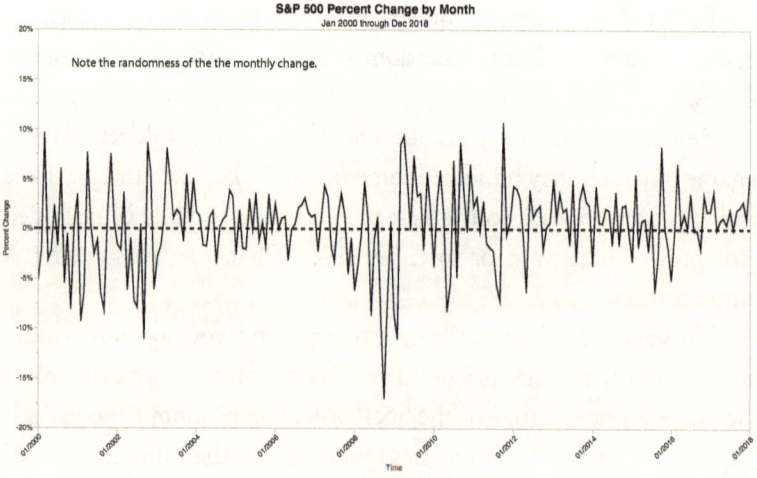

**Figure 1.2**
**Monthly Random Walk of the S&P 500**

Getting back to the efficient market hypothesis, its development started in the late 1950s with Eugene Fama, first an undergraduate student studying romance languages at Tufts University in Medford, Massachusetts. As an undergraduate, he held a job working for a professor who had a stock market forecasting service[3]. Fama's task was to devise rules for predicting equity (stock) price movements. However, his professor was a good statistician who told the young Fama to set some data aside so that he could test his rules out of sample; i.e., test the rules on data not included in the initial dataset.

Fama soon found that his rules never worked out of sample. In other words, *the rules couldn't predict equity price movements, which is what an investor truly wants.* When Fama later arrived at the University of Chicago, where he earned his PhD in economics, it occurred to him that there wasn't much predictability to stock returns because markets were working "efficiently." The hypothesis he ultimately developed resulted from this observation.

The efficient market hypothesis is an assault on much of Wall Street and more than 95 percent of all mutual funds available. Why? *Taken to its core, the efficient market hypothesis states that no one can systematically, predictably, "beat the market."* For example, in Fama's 1965 *Financial Analysts Journal* paper he stated:

> "If the random-walk theory is an accurate description of reality, then the various technical or chartist procedures for predicting stock prices are completely without value."

Fama was not ambiguous when he stated "completely without value." But he didn't stop with just the technical analysts. He also went after the other method of traditional stock analysis, which is called "fundamental" or "intrinsic value" analysis. Using this method, analysts evaluate the information available and calculate what they believe is an appropriate value for a stock. However, on this matter Fama, again in his 1965 *Financial Analysts Journal* paper, stated:

> "In an efficient market, competition among the many intelligent participants leads to a situation where, at any point in time, actual prices of individual securities

already reflect the effects of information based both on events that have already occurred and on events which, as of now, the market expects to take place in the future. In other words, in an efficient market at any point in time, the actual price of a security will be a good estimate of its intrinsic value."

He then goes on to state: ". ....on the average, competition will cause the full effects of new information on intrinsic values to be reflected instantaneously in actual prices. ...."

Although mutual fund managers have forever claimed that they can systematically beat an equal-risk portfolio of randomly selected stocks, the evidence against their claim is both longstanding and exhaustive[4,5,6].

More recent evidence exists than that cited thus far (see an example from Burton Malkiel's book cited later in this chapter), but at this point it's appropriate to establish that work supporting the efficient market hypothesis has been available and largely overlooked by investors for decades.

*As further evidence of the validity of the efficient market hypothesis, Fama received the 2015 Nobel Prize in Economics for his work regarding efficient markets,* based on 50 years of review, results, challenges and proven validity.

## The Creation of the Index Fund

Fama's work so intrigued others that they applied his findings to create something called an *index fund,* a financial product that originated through the work of American National Bank in Chicago and Wells Fargo Bank in California. Further on the subject, John C. Bogle created the first mutual fund tied to an index in 1975.

Back to mutual funds, mutual funds are either *actively* managed or *passively* managed. An actively managed fund has a fund manager who is actively buying and selling securities that he believes will provide the best financial return. With an actively managed fund or portfolio, one is betting that he, she or one's designee is smarter than the sum knowledge of all the investors in the market.

Conversely, a passively managed fund simply mimics the market. An index fund is a passively managed fund that follows a common index such as the S&P 500, which is, in the vernacular, the 500 largest companies that are traded on the American stock exchanges.

An index fund generally agrees with the efficient market hypothesis because it is betting that the markets (and thus their security prices) immediately reflect all available information. Index funds are passively managed to reflect the relative value of the companies involved (Table 1.1).

| A Personal Investment Portfolio | | |
| --- | --- | --- |
| Sample Contents: Individual stocks and bonds, mutual funds containing them and possibly other investments like CDs, gold and pork belly futures | | |
| Non-mutual Fund Investments | Mutual Funds | |
| | Types of Mutual Funds | |
| As many things as man's imagination can create, including stocks, bonds, real estate, gold, etc. | Actively managed funds (a portfolio manager picks and chooses the investments) | Passively managed funds, including index funds or market based asset funds, both of which mimic entire markets or segments of markets |

**Table 1.1**
**A Family Tree of Investments**

The composition of an index fund is straightforward and simple (Table 1.2), as each investment is proportional to the size of the company in the index, which makes for a financial product that is low cost and easy to manage. Moreover, its investments are spread across the entire economy. Hence, the product is highly diversified.

And further, the diversification is objective; i.e., it's not subject to the personal bias of a stock picker or portfolio manager.

| Assumed Index Value: | $1 Trillion | | |
|---|---|---|---|
| Assumed Portfolio Value: | $100 | | |
| Company | Assumed Company Value ($ billions) | Percent of Index | Index Fund Portfolio Investment ($100 total) |
| Microsoft | $50 | 5.0% | $5.00 |
| ExxonMobil ⟶ | $45 ⟶ | 4.5% ⟶ | $4.50 ⟶ |
| WalMart | $41 | 4.1% | $4.10 |
| ↓ | ↓ | ↓ | ↓ |
| Other companies | | | |
| ↓ | ↓ | ↓ | ↓ |
| ↓ | ↓ | ↓ | ↓ |
| ↓ | ↓ | ↓ | ↓ |
| ↓ | ↓ | ↓ | ↓ |
| ↓ | ↓ | ↓ | ↓ |
| Office Max | $1 | 0.1% | $0.10 |
| Totals | $1,000 | 100.0% | $100.00 |

**Table 1.2**
**Hypothetical Composition of a Large Company Index Fund**

Why would one manage a portfolio in this way? Because the market, being "efficient," continually adjusts to all publicly available information. In response, the index fund adjusts asset holdings frequently so that each stock is weighted according to its value in the market.

Initially, this had to be a difficult sale to investors as all the index fund seemed to be doing was mimicking the market; i.e., it seemed destined to achieve mediocrity. However, what happened has been a thorn in Wall Street's side for decades.

## The Performance of Index Fund Investments

Over the years it has become commonly known that index funds outperform peer actively managed funds. More specifically, an index fund will outperform the actively managed funds 58 to 96 percent of the time with the winning percentage generally depending on the length of the investment. In other words, the longer one holds the investment, the more likely the index fund will come out ahead.

Index funds come in all shapes and sizes: large company ("large cap" for large capitalization) index funds, small company index funds ("small cap" for small capitalization), international company index funds, bond index funds, and so forth. Hence, when we compare portfolio performance, we want to compare index funds to managed funds that have similar ingredients; i.e., that compare large company index funds to managed funds composed of large company stocks.

For the short term, should one pick an actively managed fund? No, because it's impossible to predict next year's winner[5].

Why keep the comparison among peer funds? Because different segments of a market (more on this in Chapter 2) have different risks and behave differently in the various economic cycles. Hence, for the sake of being fair and getting an explanation about what's going on in an investment portfolio, one needs to compare "apples to apples" and "oranges to oranges." Further, history has proven that each year's winning category (such as large stocks, small stocks, money market funds, long-term bonds or international stocks) follows a random-walk model.

But before forging ahead with the performance figure in mind, it will behoove us to consider what happens within an index fund. By understanding what's happening, one can optimally position himself for maximum wealth, minimum risk and lower costs.

## What's Happening in an Index Fund

One may argue that index funds are based on the total brain power involved in the market. Markets are not clairvoyant, but they do incorporate all available information almost instantaneously.

Hence, the index fund has more brain power and resources behind it than a managed fund.

Adding to the advantage of index funds is the fact that they are approximately 75 percent cheaper to operate than managed funds. Which is more expensive: (1) Programming a computer to buy and sell stocks in such a way that it follows an index? Or (2) Paying a group of highly educated portfolio managers and their supporting analysts to figure out which stocks to buy and sell? Obviously, it's much cheaper to program the computer.

How much cheaper is the index fund? On average, the operating cost to maintain an index fund is approximately 0.3 percent of the portfolio's value per year. In comparison, the average actively managed portfolio/fund costs approximately 1.3 percent of the portfolio's value per year. Where does the 1 percent cost difference end up? With an index fund it goes to the investor. With a managed fund it goes to the portfolio management and marketing teams.

While 1 percent of value may seem diminutive, it is a significant part of the difference. Why is it so significant? The S&P 500 index, what's commonly known as *"the index,"* has returned an average of approximately 10 percent per year since 1926, not including costs. When one factors in the inflation average of 3 percent, the net return is 7 percent. Hence, 1 percent equates to one-seventh of the expected return, which is a substantial advantage for the index fund.

One may argue that you need not care how much it costs to manage your money if your portfolio outperforms the market more than 1 percent. This may sound good to some, but unfortunately the thought is without grounding.

In most purchases, such as homes, cars, televisions and vacations, there is a significant relationship between what something costs and what the consumer gets. However, in the case of picking investment securities, there is little to no relationship between what something costs to manage and what the investor gets. It all goes back to Fama's efficient market/random-walk hypothesis. In summary, why should one spend more money to have a greater chance of losing?

## The Past Doesn't Predict the Future

Another common thought regarding mutual fund or stock picking is that past performance has predictive power toward future performance. However, while this may have some predictive power in other purchases, past performance has no predictive power toward future performance of publicly traded stocks and bonds.

An example of this is a table from the 1999 printing of Burton Malkiel's book, *A Random Walk Down Wall Street*[7], a best seller initially published in 1973. In his book, Malkiel, a professor at Princeton University, looked at the performance of a group of funds from 1970 to 1980, and then from 1980 to 1990. Malkiel documented the top 20 performing funds from a group of 177 from 1970 to 1980. He then compared that group to peer funds from 1980 to 1990. His findings are interesting and provide a resounding affirmation of the implications of the efficient market hypothesis. However, before looking at the results (Table 1.3), one may want to think about the business/competitive situation at hand.

The top 20 funds from 1970 to 1980 had 10 years to put their winning team together and establish a strategy for the second leg of the race, from 1980 to 1990. In a business sense, everything was going for them. The winners had ample time to assemble the team and test their methods. They likely had resources. And, seemingly even more important, the winning teams had *experience*. Logically, everything was in their favor.

From a common-sense perspective, where would you expect the winning teams to finish in the second leg of the race, from 1980 to 1990? Because the top 20 teams all performed at the 88.7th percentile or above, shouldn't they have done well in the second half? Wouldn't you expect them to all to finish at least in the top quarter of the second leg of the race? Or, how about finishing in the top half from 1980 to 1990? That should be easy. If a team finishes in the top 11.3 percent from 1970 to 1980, logically it should easily finish in the top quarter or top half from 1980 to 1990.

| Fund Name | Rank 1970-80 | Percentile | Rank 1980-90 | Percentile | Lower 50% 1980-90 |
|---|---|---|---|---|---|
| Twentieth Century Growth | 1 | 99.4 | 176 | 43.0 | * |
| Templeton Growth | 2 | 98.9 | 126 | 59.2 | |
| Quasar Associates | 3 | 98.3 | 186 | 39.8 | * |
| 44 Wall Street | 4 | 97.7 | 309 | 00.0 | * |
| Pioneer II | 5 | 97.2 | 136 | 56.0 | |
| Twentieth Century Select | 6 | 96.6 | 20 | 93.5 | |
| Security Ultra | 7 | 96.0 | 296 | 4.2 | * |
| Mutual Shares Corp. | 8 | 95.5 | 35 | 88.7 | |
| Charter Fund | 9 | 94.9 | 119 | 61.5 | |
| Magellan Fund | 10 | 94.4 | 1 | 99.7 | |
| Over-the-Counter Securities | 11 | 93.8 | 242 | 21.7 | * |
| American Capital Growth | 12 | 93.2 | 239 | 22.7 | * |
| American Capital Venture | 13 | 92.7 | 161 | 47.9 | * |
| Putnam Voyager | 14 | 92.1 | 78 | 74.8 | |
| Janus Fund | 15 | 91.5 | 21 | 93.2 | |
| Weingarten Equity | 16 | 91.0 | 36 | 88.3 | |
| Hartwell Leverage Fund | 17 | 90.4 | 259 | 16.2 | * |
| Pace Fund | 18 | 89.8 | 60 | 80.6 | |
| Acorn Fund | 19 | 89.3 | 172 | 44.3 | * |
| Stein Roe Special Fund | 20 | 88.7 | 57 | 81.6 | |

\* Bottom 10% in 1980-90 ───────────────────────────►

| Average Annual Return | | Note how the top twenty from 1970-80 didn't even beat the average from 1980-90 | | 9 of the top 20 funds from 1970-80 were in the bottom half from 1980-90 |
|---|---|---|---|---|
| Top 20 Funds | 19.0 | | 11.1 | |
| All Funds | 10.4 | | 11.7 | |
| Number of Funds | 177 | | 309 | |

**Table 1.3**
**Back to Back Performance Rankings**

From the opposite side of the argument, the efficient market hypothesis says stock price movements follow a random walk and that markets absorb and react to all publicly available information almost instantaneously. In short, the market is fast-acting on the sum knowledge of everyone investing. Hence, taking it to its core, no one should be able to systematically and predictably "beat" the market.

This is clearly a David and Goliath story. Logically, one could argue that the proven performers should easily beat the competition in the second leg of the race. However, the results, as do other studies, resoundingly endorse the efficient market hypothesis. Seventeen of the top 20 funds failed to finish in the top 10 percent from 1980-90 and performance is randomly distributed among the competitors in the second leg of the race.

What do I mean by "randomly distributed"? From the top bar chart (Figure 1.3), you can see that in the first 10 years the top 20 funds are all distributed in the top 11.3 percent of the competitors. Looking at the bottom bar chart, you'll see that one-tenth of the top twenty, or two from the first leg of the race, finished in the *bottom* 10 percent of the second leg of the race. That's amazing! Two of the funds went from the top 11.3 percent of the performers to the bottom 10 percent of the performers. Would you like to have picked these funds for 1980–90 based on their performance from 1970–80?

If we carry this logic forward, we'll see that, on average, two of the top 20 performers finished in each tenth percentile of the second leg of the race. For example, four of the 20 finished in the 80th to 90th percentile of the second leg, two of the top 20 performers finished in the 50th to 60th percentile of the race, and so on. To be sure, the second leg of the race didn't have a perfectly even distribution. Nevertheless, one can see that the performance distribution for the second 10 years is close to being random.

Three of the top 20 performers from 1970 to 1980 did finish in the top 10 percent of the competitors in the 1980 to 1990 race. Of course, the performance of these three funds was heavily marketed to take advantage of common human thought that the past predicts the future. Although the marketing pitch is based on a false premise, it's a powerfully persuasive argument, usually to the detriment of investors. In reality, on January 1, 1980, no one knew which of the twenty funds would finish in the top 10 percent, or bottom 10 percent, or any other percentile, in the next leg of the race.

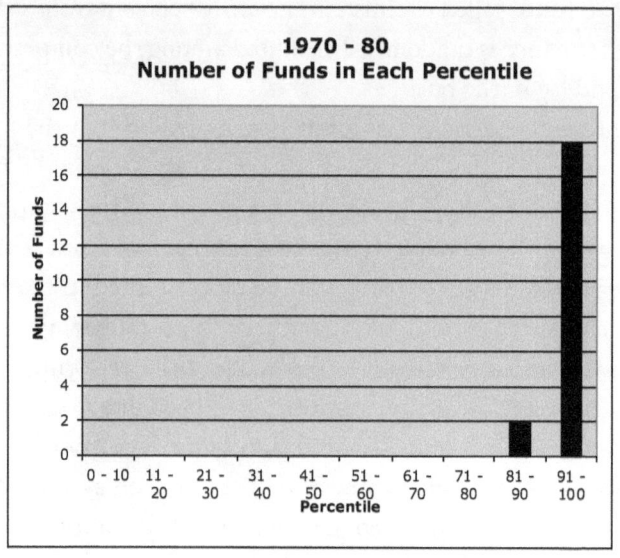

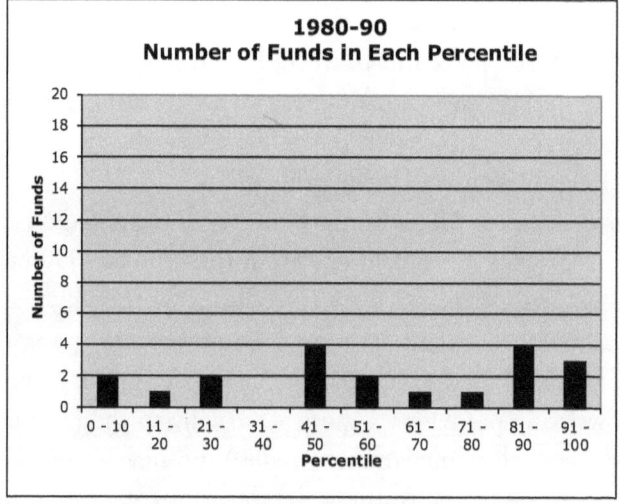

**Figure 1.3**
**Time Period Performance Comparison**

One may wonder why we're looking at data from the 1970s and 1980s instead of something more recent. It is because this phenomenon has been widely known, proven and reported for decades. Evidence for market efficiency continues to build, but the situation is nothing new. The questions this should raise include:

- Why haven't most money managers told their clients about the situation?
- Is the typical financial advisor/broker capable of understanding the facts and figures?
- Does the average financial advisor/broker inform clients of the trailers (kickbacks) he may be getting from managed funds or high-priced index funds?
- How objective is the average financial advisor/broker?
- Can the typical financial advisor/broker bring value to a client that goes beyond simply recommending mutual funds from a pre-chosen, employer-provided list?

I don't begrudge anyone making a living, especially from adult customers making free-will decisions. However, it would be good to see more investors ask questions that probe the situation. Fortunately for the investors, the word is getting out as index funds and their cousins (more on this later) have consistently taken market share away from actively managed funds for decades.

## The Government's Take on the Issue

While this may sound good from both an academic and an applied point of view, one may still wonder, what do government entities have to say about market efficiency and index funds? Not surprisingly, they have visited the issue and yes, they agree with the side supported by the facts; i.e., government entities generally support the concept of index funds usually beating their peer managed funds and that past performance does not predict future performance.

Of course, when one leaves the issue to a group of government attorneys they'll make it sound complicated. However, I'll keep it simple.

In 1992 the American Law Institute published and incorporated modern theories of investment finance into the general language of the Prudent Investor Rule[10]. Later, in 1994, the National Conference of Commissioners of Uniform State Laws passed the Uniform Prudent Investor Act (UPIA) in accordance with the Restatement of Trusts Third. This sets forth prudent fiduciary standards governing the investment conduct of trustees of private family trusts. By May 2008, 45 states, the District of Columbia and the US Virgin Islands had adopted the UPIA.

Specifically concerning efficient markets, the Prudent Investor Rule states:

> "Evidence shows that there is little correlation between fund managers' earlier successes and their ability to produce above-market returns in subsequent periods.[8]"

> "Economic evidence shows that, from a typical investment perspective, the major capital markets of this country are highly efficient, in the sense that available information is rapidly digested and reflected in the market prices of securities. As a result, fiduciaries and other investors are confronted with potent evidence that the application of expertise, investigation, and diligence in efforts to 'beat the market' in these publicly traded securities ordinarily promises little or no payoff, or even a negative payoff after taking account of research and transaction costs. Empirical research supporting the theory of efficient markets reveals that in such markets, skilled professionals have rarely been

able to identify underpriced securities (that is, to
outguess the market with respect to future return)
with any regularity.⁹"

The above is a mouthful, but the bottom line is that legal entities
have found clear enough evidence for market efficiency and the
superiority of passive investing to write it into law that has been
passed/adopted in 90 percent of the states.

## The Impact of Index Funds on the Investment Community

Because security industry companies play fast and loose with the
term "index fund," it's difficult to determine the amount of money
in true broad-based market index funds. How do companies play
"fast and loose" with the term? Mutual fund companies—loathe
to leave their active investing temptations and driven by even less
knowledgeable investors—have products such as health care index
funds, oil and gas index funds and similar investment vehicles.

Nevertheless, the amount of money in broad-based market index
funds, such as S&P 500 index funds and Russell 2000 index funds,
total in the low trillions of dollars. How significant is this to the
stock pickers of the world and their employers? It is very significant.

For example, the 1 percent difference between the cost of the
average managed fund and that of an index fund (assuming, on a
yearly basis, 1.3 percent for the managed fund and 0.3 percent for
the index fund) equates to $10 billion per year per trillion dollars
invested in index funds. Making this more specific, $10 billion
per year is enough to employ 50,000 stock pickers and investment
analysts, assuming an average cost of $200,000 per year per stock
picker/analyst. Thus, it is easy to see that the move toward index
funds has put tens of thousands of stock pickers, portfolio managers
and analysts out of work.

Is this bad, putting stock pickers out of work? No, because the money flows back to the investors, who can put it to use doing something that adds value to the economy and society. They use the money to build bigger homes, take nicer vacations, drive better cars and enjoy other goods and services that benefit the economy and put people to work.

## Why Don't More Companies Offer Index Funds?

Although market-wide index funds had an approximately 25 percent market share in 2017 and growing, they're relatively unknown and offered by a comparably small number of mutual fund companies. Why? I haven't seen a study on this, but a few common-sense explanations come to mind.

First, an index fund representing the S&P 500 should have the same investment mix as another fund representing the same index. This makes the product a commodity, reducing its competitive basis to nothing but cost and tracking performance. In short, it makes marketing the S&P 500 like marketing a bottle of ketchup. Heinz ketchup tastes the same whether it comes from Food Lion, Kroger or Walmart. The grocer's primary basis on which to compete is price. This, in turn, drives competition up and profit margins down.

Just like Heinz ketchup, an S&P 500 index fund is the same whether you buy it from Goldman Sachs, Citibank or Vanguard. Hence, mutual fund companies, investment advisors and stock brokers try to steer their customers away from low-cost alternatives that are the same no matter where they're purchased.

Second, investors have egos. If you are sitting on a sizable portfolio, you might well say, "Since I've been successful at building a sum of money, I can pick a mutual fund, or choose an investment manager, who can outperform the market."

We all have egos, and psychologists might argue that egos help to drive the creation of many good things for society. But does the average investor want his or her ego to reduce investment returns, increase risk, and raise costs? Surely not. Nevertheless, a good marketer can capitalize on the message, "You're successful. You're smart. Pick us—we'll beat the guy down the street and make you look even smarter." Or more obliquely: "Trust us, we'll make you wealthier." They may make you wealthier, but it will come with lower returns, greater risk and higher costs.

A third reason the investment community pushes managed funds, to the shortcoming of its clients and investors, is that many managed-fund products carry a fee called a trailer that flows to the salesperson. For example, if the fund has costs of 1.3 percent per year, a trailer of maybe 0.3 percent is paid to the customer's broker or financial advisor after the fund is sold, typically after an additional commission up front. Often the customer is unaware of either fee.

There's nothing wrong with making a living by selling financial advice. I do it. However, while companies can bury a 0.3 percent trailer in a 1.3 percent annual cost for a managed fund, it would be difficult to hide such a trailer in a low-cost commodity product such as an index fund. The additional cost would be readily apparent. Investors would balk at paying 0.7 percent for an S&P 500 index fund that is essentially identical to one without a trailer or up-front commission.

A fourth reason that many Wall Street firms and mutual funds companies don't offer index funds is that their top managers typically come up through the ranks as stock analysts and portfolio managers. Are they likely to admit that random chance has been a significant part of their success? Would they be willing to see their core area of expertise eliminated from their employer's business model and presumably face layoffs? In all likelihood, the answer to both questions is no.

Stock analysts and managed fund portfolio managers are generally well-educated professionals who believe in what they are doing and don't wish to short-change investors. But from the investor's point of view, the overwhelming evidence supporting the efficient market/

random-walk hypothesis strongly supports a shift in one's strategy away from active investing and toward passive investing.

## The Costs Discussed Don't Include the Broker or Advisor

It's critical to keep in mind that the costs discussed so far do NOT include the additional cost of hiring a professional broker or financial advisor. How much are these costs? They vary widely and in almost all cases they're hidden so that the investor never sees them. But, in general, they're in the range of an additional 1 percent per year.

This 1 percent may be reflected in an ongoing money management or "wrap fee," or it may come in the form of a sales commission, which is typically 5 percent up front or up to 7 percent if spread out over several years. But, overall, portfolios in the range of $100,000 to $1.5 million commonly have additional advisor/broker costs of approximately 1 percent per year if the client isn't self-servicing the account through a discount broker such as Charles Schwab or TDAmeritrade.

Hence, if you add the standard retail fees of 1.3 percent for the mutual fund and 1 percent for the broker or advisor, the total cost to the investor is in the range of 2.3 percent. Keep in mind that the average annual post-inflation return of the market is approximately 7 percent. This leaves the typical retail investor with an average real return of 4 to 5 percent.

## What About the Warren Buffets of the World?

It's true that a small number of money managers, such as Warren Buffet, have consistently beat the market over the years. However, even Warren Buffet is on record stating:

> "Most investors, both institutional and individual, will find that the best way to own common stocks is through an index fund that charges minimal fees."[10]

Further to this point, in 2009 Warren Buffet told *The Wall Street Journal*:

> "If all investors would have heeded his ideas [John Bogle's ideas advocating index funds], they would be hundreds of billions of dollars better off now,"[11]

To be sure, Warren Buffet does many things the average portfolio manager or investor can't do. One these tactics is purchasing assets that are not available in public trading, as he did with the 2002 purchase of Northern Natural Gas Pipeline. Dynegy had just purchased Northern from Enron, which was in desperate need of cash before collapsing. However, soon after purchasing Northern Natural Gas Dynegy found itself in financial straits. Thus, Buffett was able to pick up a valuable asset, Northern Natural Gas Pipeline, from Dynegy at a highly discounted price.

Buffet is not the only legendary investor to make the case for the market's efficiency and the superiority of passive investing. Peter Lynch, the famed manager of Fidelity's Magellan Fund during its storied run in the 1970s and '80s (see Table 1.3) and author of *One Up on Wall Street* and *Beating the Street*, has said that most investors would "be better off in an index mutual fund."[12]

So even some of the world's most successful stock pickers have stressed the superiority of passive over active investing for most individuals. On a cost and risk-adjusted basis, the markets yield better returns than investing with the so-called "experts."

## A Brief Discussion About Risk

Although Chapter 3 will focus exclusively on risk, it is appropriate at this point to take a step back and think about risk. With this in mind, which do you think is riskier?

> <u>Option 1:</u> Trusting your money to a group of portfolio managers and analysts who have limited knowledge of the companies they're purchasing when compared with the total brain power and resources of the market. Additionally, the group of portfolio managers and analysts may be encountering other things the average investor may not see, such as a key person leaving the portfolio team, an influential team member going through a divorce or an illness or death in the family, or general group dysfunctionality reflecting internal rivalries or personality conflicts.

> <u>Option 2:</u> Trusting your money to the general knowledge and resources of the millions of investors in the market and the trillions of dollars invested in the market.

From a qualitative standpoint, Option 2 has a lower risk than Option 1.

Bill Sharpe, Nobel Prize Laureate professor emeritus at Stanford University's Graduate School of Business and founder of FinancialEngines.com, wrote a paper in which he analytically and statistically documented that investments measured on a marketwide level have a lower risk13 than investments in actively managed funds. Hence, on a quantitative as well as qualitative basis, Option 2 is lower risk than Option 1. That's what we want: less risk, higher returns and lower costs.

## Shortcomings of Index Funds

To this point, index funds have been equated with efficient markets. Although index funds are a good starting point, one must realize their shortcomings. One shortcoming is that an index may not perfectly represent its reported market. For example, the S&P 500 may not contain the 500 largest companies in the U.S. Standard and Poor's, the company that produces the index, is a profit-driven company that sells its S&P 500 list in various forms for a variety of reasons.

Further, in putting an index together, on what basis does one define a criterion such as company size? Does it mean largest in revenue, assets, profits or market capitalization? Choosing the measurement basis can be subjective.

Another shortcoming is that an index may not appropriately represent the part of the market in which you want to invest. For example, if one invests in a Barra 600 small-cap index fund, what about the thousands of small-cap stocks that are not in the Barra 600 index? Does the index really represent them, too? Wouldn't you want to invest in peer stocks of those in the Barra 600?

Still another problem is that an index fund may buy and sell stocks slavishly to mirror the index when the change isn't enough to justify the transaction costs of buying and selling. Also, index funds are not available to investors in many 401(k) plans. In addition, there are further things an investor can do with or without index funds to optimize a portfolio.

Index funds are just that – a mutual fund that mirrors an index. They do better than peer managed funds and they are a proxy for various segments of the market. They're only a start on your journey to raise your return, reduce risk and cut costs. But, let us hope they're not the end of your journey and potential as an investor. Later chapters will discuss, in general, how you can improve on index funds.

## Managed Funds Are Not All Bad

Managed funds are not all bad, and many investors have built considerable wealth using them. In fact, since managed funds have the large majority of the market, most investors have built their wealth through actively managed portfolios. If you look at Table 1.3 you'll see that the average return of the subject funds in the second leg of the race was 11.1 percent. Who would be disappointed with 11.1 percent per year over a 10-year period? Although one may not get the average return of the market or even the average return of all managed funds, following a disciplined and reasonable investment strategy over the decades can still build considerable wealth.

Further, other limitations may preclude one from pursuing a passive fund investment strategy. One of these limitations may be what's available in your 401(k) plan. The 401(k) is the primary investment vehicle of most Americans, and if index funds or market-based asset funds are not available, the investor must choose from actively managed funds.

Another limitation that may preclude pursuing a passive investment strategy is the investor's tax situation. Passively managed funds generally have a lower tax liability than actively managed funds, but the investor may have already accumulated significant gains in actively managed positions. Therefore, converting a managed fund position to a passive fund position may not be wise because of the tax liability incurred.

## "I Buy Stocks Because I Don't Believe in Mutual Funds. ...."

While some investors may say "I buy stocks because I don't believe in mutual funds," this view is naïve and obtuse. If you are purchasing stocks for your own account, you have the equivalent of a closed-end, actively managed investment fund, or, in other words, a fund that differs from a mutual fund only in that it's open to one investor and not the entire public.

Of course, the self-directed stock picker may claim to save on expenses. This, too, is a bit naïve. If you have earned (as opposed to inherited) the money necessary to make a significant stock investment, you will earn far more per hour pursuing your trade than you will save researching stocks and managing your portfolio instead of just buying into an index fund or market based fund. Keep in mind that it's not just about return, but how much return per unit of risk, as discussed later.

## A Macroeconomic Case for the Superiority of Market Efficiency

One can also see tangible evidence of the superiority of market efficiency on a macro scale by briefly reviewing 20th century history.

The Soviet Union was established following the 1917 Russian Revolution, and a communist economic system was imposed. This led to prices of essentially everything being set by the government rather than the market. Following the doctrines of Marx and Lenin, government officials determined what they thought was the correct price of a bushel of wheat, a pair of shoes or anything else and in so doing believed they were creating a society that would be superior to one based on capitalism and market based prices. In essence, they assumed their wisdom exceeded that of the free market.

However, in the many turbulent decades that followed, the Soviet Union never achieved the economic efficiency of the world's most developed countries with more market-oriented economies. Shortages of goods and services were endemic. Even in its best years, living standards in the Soviet Union—and the other countries that adopted communism—remained well below those in the world's leading capitalist economies. Ultimately, the Soviet economy collapsed and the practice of the government setting prices gave way to a more market-driven system.

While we don't think of stock pickers resembling Soviet bureaucrats, the fact is that stock pickers display their own type of belief in their ability to outperform the market in determining the appropriate price of a stock. Because of the random, unpredictable movement of security prices, stock pickers sometimes do outperform the market. And when they do their marketing departments make sure we hear about the funds that "beat the market." With thousands, or even millions, of stock pickers playing the game, some will beat the market for multiple years running. But it's like rolling dice. If thousands of people play the game, someone will roll four sevens in a row and claim they knew *a priori* that they "were hot." However, as with gambling statistics, there is extensive evidence showing that stock movements are random and the market is efficient.

## Going Forward

Are index funds and the efficient market hypothesis the only things one needs to know about managing our portfolio? No. It's just a solid start, a foundation. Decades of excellent portfolio optimizing strategies and tactics have been developed and proven. Understanding and applying these strategies and tactics will raise your return, reduce your risk and cut your cost. Fortunately, the simple information contained in this and later chapters is quick to learn and easy to understand. These strategies and tactics will reduce the time you need to set aside for managing your finances so that you can devote your time and energy to enjoying life and not worrying about your investments. The strategies and tactics will also enable better financial forecasting, thus yielding additional benefits.

1.  Fama, Prices," *Financial Analysts Journal*, September–October 1965.
2.  Fama, "The Behavior of Stock Market Prices," *Journal of Business*, January 1965.
3.  The Federal Reserve Bank of Minneapolis, *Interview with Eugene Fama*, interview conducted on November 2, 2007 and posted on www.minneapolisfed.org.
4.  "A Study of Mutual Funds," prepared by the Wharton School of Finance and Commerce for the Securities and Exchange Commission. Report of the Committee on Interstate and Foreign Commerce. Washington: U.S. Government Printing Office (1962).
5.  John C. Bogle, *The Little Book of Common Sense Investing*, pages 30–34, John Wiley and Sons, 2007.
6.  Larimore, Lindauer and LeBoeuf, *The Bogleheads' Guide to Investing*, page 166, John Wiley & Sons, Inc., 2006.
7.  Burton Malkiel, *A Random Walk Down Wall Street*, page 183, W.W. Norton & Company, 1999 (previous printings in 1973, 1975, 1981, 1985, 1990 and 1996).
8.  Restatement 3rd of Trusts (Prudent Investor Rule), page 75.
9.  Edward C. Halbach, Jr., the Reporter for the Restatement 3rd of Trusts and Walter Perry Johnson professor of law emeritus at the University of California law school, in "Trust Investment Law in the Third Restatement," *Real Property, Probate and Trust Journal*, Volume 27, Fall 1992, pages 407–65; see Reporter's General Note on Section 227 of the Restatement 3rd of Trusts (Prudent Investor Rule), comments e through h, page 79.
10. Warren Buffet, legendary stock picker, in the Chairman's Letter, 1996 Berkshire Hathaway Corporation Annual Report.
11. "John C. Bogle, Founder of Vanguard Group, Dies at 89," *The Wall Street Journal*, January 17, 2019.
12. Peter Lynch, "Is there Life After Babe Ruth?" *Barron's*, April 2, 1990, page 15.
13. William F. Sharpe, *The Styles and Performance of Large Seasoned U.S. Funds 1985–94*, published on the worldwide web, March 1995.

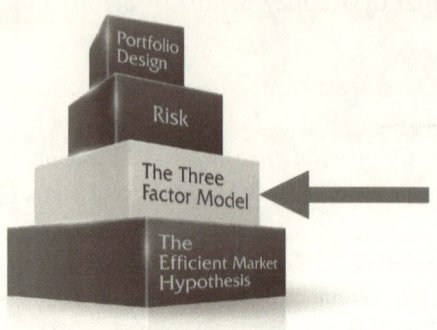

## CHAPTER 2

# The Three-Factor Model

*Focusing on What Matters the Most*

**Unconventional Wisdom**
*Did you know that three simple factors explain approximately 90 percent of a portfolio's return? And none of the key factors are the portfolio manager or its past performance. What are they? Read on, as it's surprisingly common-sensical....*

Because we know from Chapter 1 that the market is efficient, is there anything one can do besides buy an index fund or a market-based asset fund? Absolutely. The next logical step is to look at what truly impacts a portfolio. If you know what makes a difference, you can adjust your portfolio to improve your return per unit of risk (more on risk in Chapter 3).

## The Three-Factor Model

In general, the Fama-French Three-Factor Model evolved from a series of papers[1,2,3,4,5] and gets somewhat complicated. However, its ultimate findings are rather simple. Approximately 90 percent of a portfolio's return can be explained by the following three factors:

- Stocks vs. bonds
- Small stocks vs. large stocks
- Value stocks vs. growth stocks

It is critical to understand that these factors don't *predict* a portfolio's return. No one and no model is clairvoyant. However, the above three factors, used together, can explain the bulk of a portfolio's return. This gives you another tool to use in building an optimal portfolio that best fits your risk tolerance, time horizon and investment objectives.

## Return of the Stock Market *minus* the "Risk-Free Return"

If you lump all the stocks in the market together and calculate the return over a given period, say a year, you have the overall return of the market, which is mathematically referred to as *Rm*. Why is this important to a stock portfolio's return? Because stocks statistically are highly correlated, i.e., they tend to rise and fall together.

In contrast to the return of the market, which has risk, there is the "risk-free" return of the treasury bill, which is mathematically referred to as *Rf*. Why is the treasury bill considered "risk-free"? Because it is a short-term loan to the government, backed by the complete taxing power of the government. The risk-free assumption might be debatable in connection with some governments. However, the market generally believes that if the government involved is stable, any risk is minimal because treasury bills have such short maturities.

From this one has the difference between the two variables, Rm – Rf, which is the difference between the return of the overall stock market and the return on the risk-free treasury bill. In academic parlance, one can say that **Rm – Rf is the *risk premium* the investor gets for holding a stock** instead of a short-term loan to a stable government. Thus we have the stocks vs. bonds factor.

## Small Stocks vs. Large Stocks

Historically, **small stocks have delivered higher returns than large stocks**. Why? The full answer is beyond the scope of this book, but it is useful to consider a few things when comparing the returns of small stocks to large stocks. These are largely common-sense observations.

- Small companies have a higher risk of financial mortality or loss than large companies. The higher risk commands a higher cost of capital to the company and thus causes it to set a higher hurdle rate of return for the investments it makes to run the business. Therefore, small companies will likely have higher returns than large companies.
- Small companies are likely to be less diversified than large companies and thus likely to have more volatile, higher risk cash flow streams than large companies. These factors will be reflected in a stock that has greater risk and volatility.
- Small companies are often able to react more quickly to changing market conditions in their industry and thus are more profitable than large companies. Hence, they usually grow faster than large companies, and this difference will be reflected in their stock returns compared with those of large companies.

Again, the above are just general considerations. What is important is that small stocks tend to outperform large stocks over the long term. The tendency of small stocks to outperform large stocks is well documented and highly recognized. Hence, it will behoove you to accept this part of the three-factor model and incorporate it in your portfolio.

## Value Stocks vs. Growth Stocks

Before going further into the science and accounting of the matter, I'm going to make this real simple. The academics may not like this, but value vs. growth is simple if you keep the following in mind:

1) Don't be swayed by the term "growth" in your investing.
2) Imagine selling ALL of a company's assets and comparing the resulting pile of cash to the presale value of ALL of the company's stock, or dollars per share times the total number of shares outstanding. Then, by definition:
   a. The asset sale "pile of cash" from a "value" company, <u>compared with</u> the "pile of cash" it would have gotten from selling all of its stock, will be higher than the "pile of cash" from a "growth" company, <u>compared with</u> the "pile of cash" it would have gotten from selling all of *its* stock. *Or*
   b. To make it even simpler, "value" companies own more assets compared with their stock value than "growth" companies.

To dive a bit deeper so that you can better understand the situation, consider the following two definitions:

*Book Equity* (BE) is the value of a company's assets if liquidated.

*Market Equity* (ME) is the total value of a company's outstanding shares of stock; i.e., the number of shares outstanding times the dollar price per share of stock.

As summarized by Fama and French, stocks with a low book equity to market equity (BE/ME) ratio are considered "growth" stocks, whereas stocks with a high BE/ME ratio are considered "distressed" stocks, also known as "value" stocks. But ironically, high BE/ME, or "distressed," stocks tend to have a higher return and less volatility than low BE/ME stocks. Thus, **value stocks tend to outperform growth stocks,** on their own and per unit of risk, although that can vary.

By investment accounting definition, half of all stocks are "value" stocks and half are "growth" stocks.

Do stocks change from "value" to "growth" and vice versa? Absolutely, every day. In fact, the change is taking place every moment of every day as stock prices go up and down. Those stocks that are close to the border between value and growth are crossing back and forth over the line. Figure 2.1 may help to explain the situation.

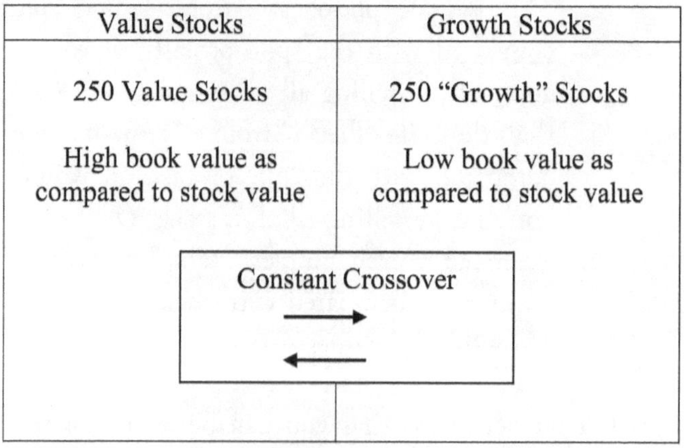

| Value Stocks | Growth Stocks |
|---|---|
| 250 Value Stocks | 250 "Growth" Stocks |
| High book value as compared to stock value | Low book value as compared to stock value |

Constant Crossover
→
←

**Figure 2.1**
**S&P 500 Value vs. Growth Matrix**

Does this mean that investors should only buy value stocks and avoid growth stocks because returns on value stocks tend to outperform those on growth stocks? No, because growth stocks represent half the economy and one shouldn't ignore a segment that large. However, *investors should tilt their portfolios toward value for optimal return per unit of risk, while maintaining a sizable amount of growth stocks.*

## The 2014-2019 Growth Stock Run-Up

Historically, over multi-year time periods, Value stocks have outperformed Growth stocks. However, with the rapid and sizable growth of Facebook, Amazon, Alphabet/Google, Apple, Microsoft and possibly some other tech companies such as Netflix, Growth stocks have outperformed Value stocks to the point that even on long term horizons, such as the last 10-20 years, Growth is ahead of Value. Does this mean that one should discard the Value vs. Growth implications of the Three Factor Model?

To answer this, I believe one needs to look a bit deeper into the situation. First, keep in mind that, between early 2014 and the middle of 2019, Facebook grew 3.5 times from $55 to $190 per share, Amazon grew 4.75 times from $400 to $1900 per share, Alphabet/Google doubled from $550 to $1100 per share, Apple grew 2.5 times from $80 to $200 per share and Microsoft grew 3.7 times from $37 to $135 per share. In short, this group of tech companies tripled their total market capitalization from $1.5 trillion to $4.5 trillion in less than six years. That's staggering!

By comparison, over this same period of time, the S&P 500 index (SPX) grew 1.6 times from $1820 to $2950 per share. That's not bad (and much of that growth was from Silicon Valley), but it's nowhere near the growth of the tech companies over the same period of time. The total market capitalization of the S&P 500 on June 30, 2019 was $25.6 trillion. So, in other words, the subject five companies, or 1 percent of the S&P 500 companies, account for 18 percent of the value of the S&P 500.

Digging a bit deeper, the aforementioned tech companies have minimal assets other than software (code), some server farms (stocked with hardware that is typically obsolete in three years), the shipping warehouses of Amazon and stockpiles of cash. They have minimal factories, inventory, real estate or other hard assets. Also, their brand value can be severely damaged by a competitor with a turn of technology. Does anyone remember the one-time dominance of Novell Networks or Yahoo? Almost by definition, what tech companies do have becomes largely obsolete in a few years. Additionally, an expensive arsenal of employees burn through substantial amounts of cash on a daily basis.

In comparison, think of McDonald's with its thousands of restaurants and products that never grow obsolete (yes, the food spoils in a few days but customers get hungry every few hours). The real estate value of the restaurants is staggering, as well as the ubiquitous golden arches. Yes, the hard assets may be largely owned by franchisees, but their hands are tied to the corporation in multiple ways. It's a never-ending cash flow machine with substantial assets, both hard and soft.

Similarly, ExxonMobil has thousands of producing oil wells and billions of barrels of proven oil reserves in the ground. Electric automobiles may ultimately replace gasoline powered vehicles, but the laws of thermodynamics, combined with industry infrastructure, will prevent such a change from happening rapidly.

And over on the health care side of things, Quest Diagnostics, for example, has strategically located labs, contracts with hospitals, clinics and physicians, billions of dollars in equipment and a continuous supply of people needing health care.

Google may have billions of users looking for Internet search help, but their revenue is largely based on advertising and their technology has a short shelf life before becoming obsolete. Supplanting Google is as easy as typing something else in a computer's search bar (I now use Duck Duck Go almost exclusively for privacy reasons). Similarly, Apple contracts close to 100 percent of its manufacturing and simply rents the majority of the space for its retail stores. To be sure, I don't expect the tech companies to go away anytime soon, but they have minimal hard assets and they're on a fast-paced treadmill that can unexpectedly throw them off at any time.

Thus, in summary, Growth stocks have outperformed Value stocks substantially over the past few years. However, I would be hesitant to tilt the equity side of a portfolio toward Growth stocks instead of Value stocks. Because the capital markets are split 50/50, by definition, between Value and Growth, one needs to own both. Nevertheless, for the purpose of steadily building personal wealth and keeping risk in check, one is probably better off to have a portfolio that's tilted more toward Value stocks than Growth stocks.

## Investment Costs and the Three-Factor Model

Logically, you should put your money toward what makes the biggest difference. Because the aforementioned three factors account for approximately 90 percent of a portfolio's return, the potentially hundreds of other factors make a total impact of only about 10 percent. Hence, when it comes to assembling a portfolio, you should focus most of your time, expense and investment decision making, in order of importance, on:

1) Stocks vs. bonds
2) Value vs. growth
3) Small vs. large

Sadly, most investors and financial advisors focus most of their time and funds on things that make a comparatively small difference on portfolio return, including the mutual fund company, which industries to select, the portfolio manager and any number of other factors.

Regarding costs, from Chapter 1, managed funds typically have a cost of 1.3 percent per year, vs. 0.3 percent per year for index or asset-based funds (more on asset-based funds, which are similar to index funds, later). Therefore, approximately 77 percent of the cost (1/1.3) was for active fund management, which is a factor that doesn't matter much. This begs the question:

*Does it make sense to spend 77 percent of one's investment cost on things that account for less than 10 percent of the return?*

Definitely not! If 77 percent of your cost is not even remotely related to 77 percent of your return, you should seek an alternative investment in which time and money are not allocated to areas with little impact on your return.

## Summary

Because of the three-factor model and the efficient market hypothesis, you can ignore most of the financial "news" that you see and hear because it makes little or no difference to your portfolio. The primary driver of most financial news is to sell the publication.

Similarly, and sadly, most investment advisors and stock brokers steer their clients' attention toward information that has little or no impact on the factors that affect their return on investment. Research indicates that people make decisions on emotions and then look for facts to support their decisions. Thus, most investment advisors, like most newscasters, are very good at managing and guiding human emotions. Sadly, for both professions, it's what pays the most.

However, what pays for the bills and the lifestyle of the investor is the investment value. Thus, investors should be wary of their emotions and focus on well-grounded elements that are solidly related to their investment return—the efficient market hypothesis and the three-factor model. These are the things that will determine whether the investor will have the necessary financial resources to take their children and grandchildren on the cruise or other vacation of their choice.

We would all like to be clairvoyant, but that's beyond our ability. Nevertheless, we can make our investment decisions on that which we know will likely explain most of the return we will achieve. And by applying this information, we can better predict the future value of our portfolios. This isn't clairvoyance; rather, it's prudent investing and smart planning.

The good news is that you only need to understand three things to explain approximately 90 percent of your return and take the initial steps toward designing your portfolio. These three things are:

1) Stocks vs. bonds
2) Value vs. growth
3) Small vs. large

Focusing on these three factors, combined with the efficient market hypothesis as discussed in Chapter 1, will get you a long way down the road to optimizing your portfolio. The next logical thing to discuss is risk, as we live in an uncertain world and every investor needs to understand and manage the risks he or she is taking.

1.  Eugene F. Fama and Kenneth R. French, "The Cross-Section of Expected Stock Returns," *The Journal of Finance*, June 1992.
2.  Fischer Black, "Beta and Return," *The Journal of Portfolio Management*, Fall 1993.
3.  Eugene F. Fama and Kenneth R. French, "Common Risk Factors in the Returns on Stocks and Bonds," *Journal of Financial Economics* **33**:3–56, 1993.
4.  Eugene F. Fama and Kenneth R. French, "Value versus Growth: the International Evidence," *The Journal of Finance*, December 1998.
5.  James L. Davis, Eugene F. Fama and Kenneth R. French, "Characteristics, Covariances and Average Returns: 1929 to 1997," *The Journal of Finance*, February 2000.

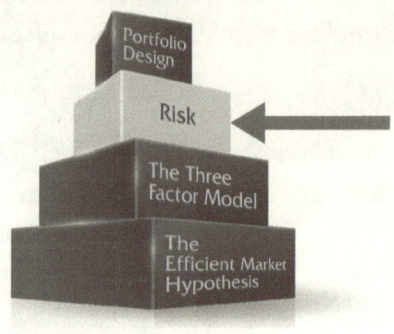

## CHAPTER 3

# Risk

*Do you care about what you stand to gain or lose?*

> **Unconventional Wisdom**
> *If you invest $100,000 today, don't you want to know the chance of it being $85,000 a year from now? You may not want to think of this, but it's better to know the facts up front than to deal with unpleasant results later. Risk is something you can measure and a reality you need to deal with. Read on to find out more...*

What comes to your mind when you hear the word, risk? Answers to this question commonly range from "losing all my money" to "necessary to make a lot of money." You're probably somewhere between these two extremes.

By accepting ***uncertainty*** as a simple definition of risk, one can make rapid progress on the issue. To be sure, uncertainty isn't a perfect or all-encompassing definition, but using it as a simple definition will allow us to rapidly move forward in understanding portfolio behavior and design. More specifically, accepting uncertainty as a definition of risk will allow you to apply mathematical rigor, very simply, to the situation. And even more important, as you gain experience with this application and practice you'll likely find that managing the uncertainty of your portfolio will help you sleep well at night while still allowing you to move toward your financial goals.

## Statistics 101 for Fun and Profit

Before diving into Statistics 101, do you know who invented the subject, when he invented it or most importantly, WHY he invented it?

Girolamo Cardano, an Italian, invented the subject in the 16th century[1]. But why did he invent statistics? Gambling. To be specific, Cardano investigated probability, a close cousin of statistics. Nevertheless, personal financial gain was the driving force behind his study.

Does this sound a bit like Las Vegas? To make an overly simple analogy, investing with the principles discussed in this book will move you from the position of being a gambler going to Las Vegas to the position of owning a casino in Las Vegas. These principles put the statistics to work in favor of you instead of against you. In short, what we discuss in this chapter, combined with what's presented in the other chapters, will convert common headwinds into tailwinds that will enable you to systematically build your wealth.

Going back to the casino analogy, many investors can't resist the temptation to gamble with their investments and partake of the short-term sugar high it creates. Hence, most investors choose the position of being the gambler instead of the casino owner and then wonder, 30 years down the road, why they're both frustrated and near broke, with minimal or negative returns on their investments. However, there is a better way to invest, but to get there you need to understand a few things about risk, and thus the need to have a simple understanding of statistics.

## A Simple Golfing Example

Rather than launching into formulas and other abstract thoughts, just take a minute and consider two golfers, John and Sam. They have the same average score, 95. However, John is much more consistent than Sam, as John has a *standard deviation* of 2 strokes, while Sam, who has a strong drive but an unpredictable hook, has a *standard deviation* of 6 strokes. Stick with me and don't get lost on the term *standard deviation*. We'll make it easy, real easy.

If you had to predict what each golfer will shoot tomorrow, your answer is easy: 95, because they each have an average of 95.

However, if your cousin Lenny, an avid golf spectator, asked you:

"What *range* do you expect John to shoot between?" Your answer would still be easy, as you would remember from reading *Great Minds, Great Wealth*: "I'm 95-percent certain that John will shoot between a 91 and a 99".

How can you get such a quick answer? It's easy. An average plus and minus two standard deviations covers a 95 percent certainty range. Conversely, the average plus or minus one standard deviation covers only a 68 percent certainty range. That's a mouthful, but it's critical, so please take a moment to read it again (Table 3.1).

| Golfer | Average ("Mean") Score | Standard Deviation | 95% Confidence Interval (we're 95% certain that tomorrow's score will land between these two figures) |
|---|---|---|---|
| John | 95 | 2 strokes | **91 – 99** (95 – 2 std devs x 2 strokes = 91, And 95 + 2 std devs x 2 strokes = 99) |
| Sam | 95 | 6 strokes | **83 – 107** (95 – 2 std devs x 6 strokes = 83, And 95 + 2 std devs x 6 strokes = 107) |

**Table 3.1**
**Illustration of Golf Score Confidence Interval**

Going back to being 95-percent confident John will shoot between 91 and 99, it's 95, his average, plus or minus two standard deviations, which is 95 plus or minus four (2 x 2). This gives you a *95 percent confidence interval* of 91 to 99, with an expected average of 95. Thus, 95 is the middle, or peak, of the bell curve (Figure 3.1a). John is obviously a very consistent golfer.

On the other hand, what if Lenny asked:

"What range do you expect Sam to shoot between?"

Remembering that Sam has a standard deviation of 6 strokes, you'd immediately reply:

"I'm 95 percent certain that Sam will shoot between an 83 and a 107". Once again, how did we get 83 and 107? 95 (Sam's average) minus two standard deviations (2 x 6 = 12) is 83, while 95 plus two standard deviations (2 x 6 = 12) equals 107 (Figure 3.1b). Wow. Sam is not nearly as consistent as John. When Sam is hot he can blister the course, but when Sam has an off day it can be miserable.

Because you may do better with pictures than words, you may want to briefly look at the bell curves for John and Sam. In short, the higher the standard deviation/uncertainty, the flatter the bell curve (Sam). Conversely, the lower the standard deviation/uncertainty, the steeper the bell curve (John).

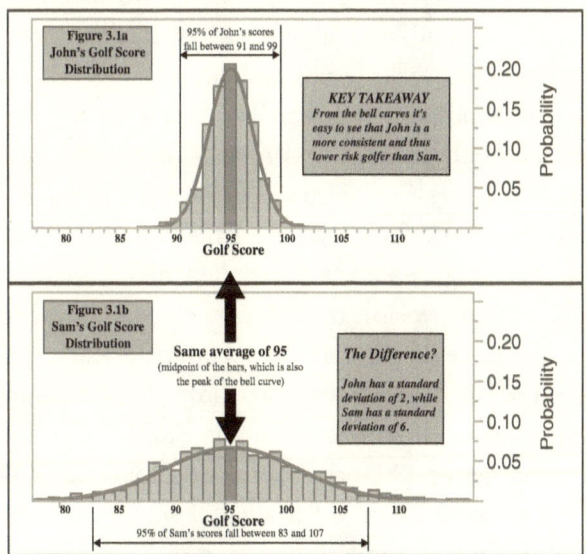

**Figures 3.1a and 3.1b**
**Bell Curves of John's and Sam's Golf Scores**

*The Take Away:*
*John is a more consistent, more certain golfer than Sam, as*
*John has a lower standard deviation than Sam*

If both John and Sam had a fan club, which club do you think incurs more heartburn: John's or Sam's? Sam's fan club will likely suffer more heartburn than John's because Sam's scores are not as consistent as John's scores. They both have the same average (95), but John is far more predictable than Sam.

At this point you can relax, as this is as technical as we'll get regarding statistics. The rest is easy, as we'll just move the golf score example over to your portfolio and use dollars instead of golf strokes. But again, relax, as it's as easy as the preceding example.

## The Link Between Golf Scores and Your Portfolio

Do you remember back in Chapter 2 how three things explain approximately 90 percent of a portfolio's return? Two of those factors, stocks vs. bonds and large stocks vs. small stocks, are easy to explain. In short, stocks return more than bonds because stocks are *riskier* than bonds. Similarly, small stocks return more than large stocks because small stocks are *riskier* than large stocks.

Applying what we learned from our discussion of golf scores and standard deviation, stocks are more volatile (uncertain) than bonds and thus have a higher standard deviation than bonds. Likewise, small stocks are more volatile than large stocks, and their prices have a higher standard deviation than that of large stocks.

Putting the numbers to a few portfolios will give us some actual figures. Specifically, domestic small cap stocks have an annual standard deviation of 18.1 percent, the S&P 500 (large domestic stocks) has an annual standard deviation of 16.6 percent, long term bonds have an annual standard deviation of 7.9 percent and U.S. Short Term Government Bonds have an annual standard deviation of

6.4 percent (Table 3.2). Similarly, as one decreases risk, the geometric average return decreases from 14.1 percent for domestic small cap stocks to 6.5 percent for U.S. short term government bonds. Risk and return move together, as you go from the high-risk, high-return small stocks to the low-risk, low-return short-term government bonds.

To further illustrate the point, the riskiest asset on Table 3.2, small cap stocks, have logically both the worst one-year performance (-36.9 percent) and the best one-year performance (54.0 percent). Moreover, the lowest risk asset in the table, short-term government bonds, have the least negative worst year (-1.8 percent), and the lowest return best year (28.0 percent). Again, risk and return are related.

| Asset Class | Geometric Average Return | Arithmetic Average Return | | Standard Deviation | | Worst | Best |
|---|---|---|---|---|---|---|---|
| U.S. Small Cap Blend¹ | 14.1% | 15.6% | Increasing Return | 18.1% | Increasing Std Dev & Risk | -36.9% | 54.0% |
| S&P 500¹ | 11.5% | 13.4% | | 16.6% | | -36.6% | 37.2% |
| Long Term Bonds¹ | 8.3% | 8.6% | | 7.9% | | -5.8% | 34.2% |
| U.S. Short Term Government Bonds¹ | 6.5% | 6.7% | | 6.4% | | -1.8% | 28.0% |

**Table 3.2**
**Asset Class Investment Performance from 1975–2014**
*Past performance does not predict future performance*

However, reflecting back on Chapter 1, security prices follow a "random-walk" model and no one is clairvoyant. Hence, on January 1 of any given year, no one knows which asset class will have the best return for the coming 12 months. But, over a long-term, multiyear period, one can expect the riskier asset classes to have, on average, a higher return than the lower risk asset classes.

Rather than just trying to interpret a table full of numbers, a picture of the bell curves for various, significantly different risk asset classes may help you understand the situation a bit better. Remember, narrow bell curves have a lower standard deviation than flat bell curves because narrow bell curves represent a lower standard deviation than the flat bell curves. The flatter the bell curve, the higher the risk/uncertainty (Figure 3.2, expected returns and standard deviations rounded to the nearest percent. Also, note that three of the four asset classes in Figure 3.2 are different than those in Table 3.2).

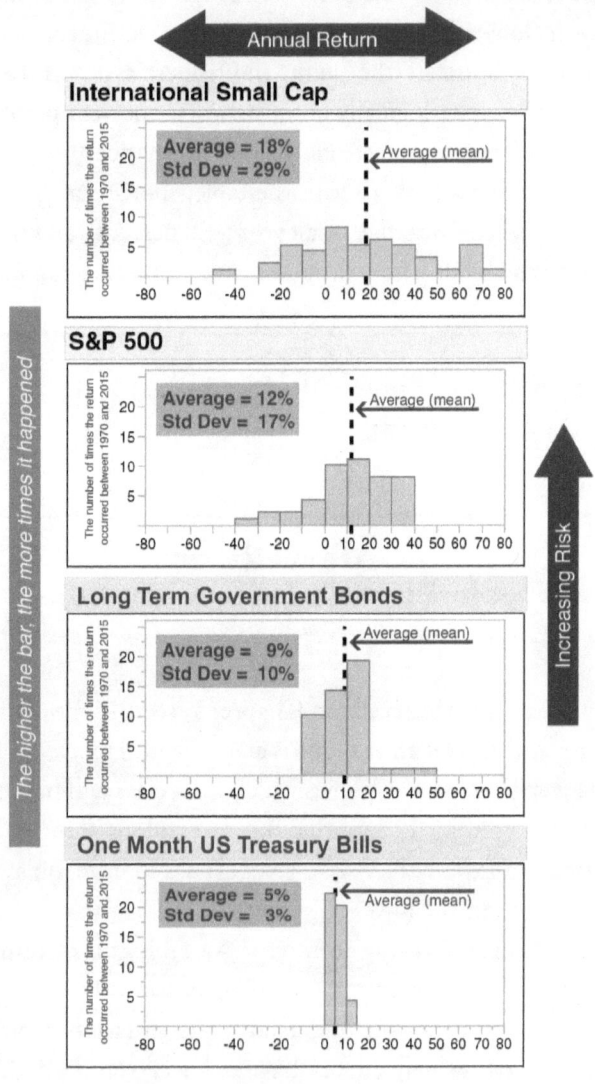

**Figure 3.2**
**Bell Curves for Various Investments from 1975-2014**
*Past performance does not predict future performance*

In looking at the bell curves, it's also important to notice that **the peak of the bell curve**, which occurs at the average of the data represented, **shifts to the right as we move up the risk continuum.** In other words, as we move from low-risk investments toward high-risk investments, from the bottom to the top, the average return increases. The bell curves graphically illustrate the relationship between risk and return in both shape (flatness, steepness and density of the bell curve data) and the location of the peak of the bell curve. Summarizing, for the case of investment options:

- Flat bell curve: Higher risk, peak is further to the right
- Steep bell curve: Lower risk, peak is further to the left

Of course, the holy grail of investing is a steep bell curve with a peak that's way off to the right. This equates to a high return with minimal risk, which is what corporations, entrepreneurs and venture capitalists are always looking for.

## Fitting the Bell Curves to Your Situation

Having learned about standard deviation and the relationship between risk and return, the next question is, "How does this fit into my investment portfolio and personal financial goals?" Once again, it's easiest to answer the question with an example.

Suppose you're an investment advisor and your client, Susie, whose investment portfolio is 100 percent in the S&P 500, asks you: "My portfolio value today is $100,000. What will it be in a year, neglecting investment expenses?"

In reflecting on Susie's question we need to recognize three things:

- You don't know what the return will be for the coming year. Stock price movements follow a random-walk pattern and the market is efficient.

- Although we don't know what next year's return will be, we can make a statement about the *expected* return and *probable range* of the return.
- By knowing an expected return and probable range of the return, we can give Susie an expected value of the portfolio and a range into which it is likely to fall at the end of the year.

Applying these three points we can draw the following:

Because the mean arithmetic return, or peak of the bell curve, is 11.5 percent (second chart from the top of Figure 3.2, where 11.5% was rounded up to 12%), the return multiplier is 1.115 (1.000 + 11.5/100). Therefore, the *expected value* of Susie's domestic large-cap value portfolio, neglecting investment costs, is:

$$\$100,000 \times 1.115 = \mathbf{\$111,500}$$

However, this is an uncertain estimate because the market follows a random walk and returns are uncertain. Further, the bell curve for the S&P 500 is very flat because the S&P 500 is, as true of almost any equity investment, volatile. Nevertheless, because the standard deviation for the S&P 500 is 16.6 percent (again, Table 3.2), one can be 95 percent certain the value of her portfolio in one year will be:

Expected Range = $111,500 +/- 2 standard deviations

And because the standard deviation is 16.6 percent, we know that 2 standard deviations equate to **$33,200** ($100,000 x 2 x 0.166)

Therefore, Susie can be 95-percent certain the portfolio value after one year, neglecting investment costs, will be $111,500 +/- **$33,200**

This yields:

- A low value of $78,300 ($111,500 – 33,200)
- A high value of $144,700 ($111,500 + $33,200)

Keep in mind, the expected value, or midpoint of Susie's investment value bell curve, is $111,500. Thus, even a simple basket of "blue chip" companies has a wide potential outcome range (Figure 3.3).

## S&P 500 Expected Return

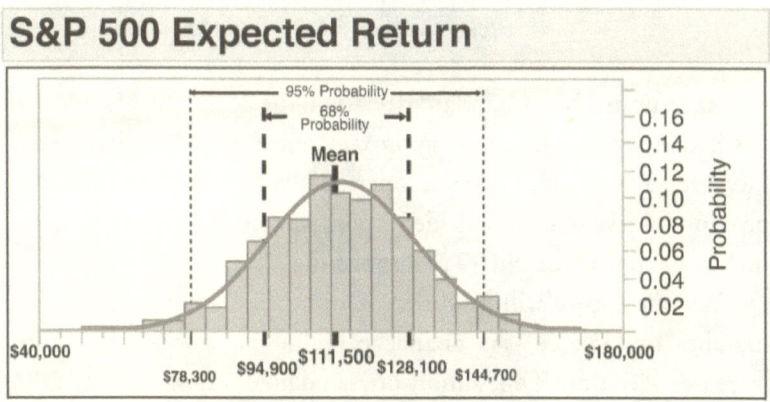

**Figure 3.3**
**Potential Range of Susie's S&P 500**
**Portfolio Value After One Year**

Summarizing the answer to Susie's question about her S&P 500 portfolio value in one year (Figure 3.3) we have:

- We don't know what the value of her portfolio will be in one year because stock market returns follow a random-walk model (Chapter 1). However, we can state the following:
  - o The most likely, or expected, value for the portfolio one year from today is $111,500.
  - o We're 95-percent certain the value one year from today will be above $78,300 and below $144,700.
    - ▪ A 95-percent certainty is equivalent to a 19-out-of-20 chance that the result will end *within* this range.

o We're 68-percent certain (one standard deviation) the portfolio's value, in one year, will be above $94,900 and below 128,100.

- A 68-percent certainty is equivalent to an almost one-out-of-three chance that the result will end *outside of* this range.

As indicated by its standard deviation, the S&P 500, historically, has had a negative return in approximately one out of three years. However, again from a historical perspective, holding the S&P 500 position for five years has yielded a positive return (not counting for inflation) approximately 90 percent of the time.

Yes, the future will be different from the past, but capitalism marches on. Hence, the chance of achieving a positive return increases with time if one simply buys and holds on to the S&P 500.

Suppose that, after looking at the wide range of potential outcomes for a portfolio holding the S&P 500, Susie asks: "What happens if I go the ultrasafe route and just hold one month U.S. Treasury Bills for a year?"

Fortunately, we know an investment in one month U.S. Treasury Bills has an expected return of 3.5 percent (which equates to $3,500 on an investment of $100,000) and a standard deviation of 3.2 percent (both figures based on the 1930-2015 arithmetic mean). Thus, using the same methodology as for the S&P 500, we have:

- An expected value of $103,500 after one year
- A 95-percent certainty range of $103,500 +/- 2 x $3,200 (3.2 percent of $100,000), which yields a low value of $97,100 and a high value of $109,900.
- A 68-percent certainty range of $103,500 +/- $3,200, or $100,300 to $106,700.

Based on this data, the treasury bill bell curve is steeper and narrower than the bell curve for the S&P 500 (Figure 3.4).

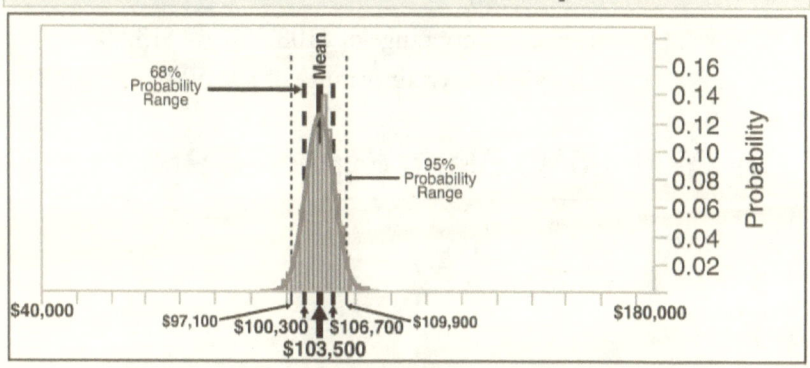

# One Month U.S. Treas Bill Exp Return

**Figure 3.4**
**Potential Range Susie's Treasury Bill**
**Investment After One Year**

However, let's assume that after Susie looks at the two options, the S&P 500 vs. the one-month U.S. Treasury Bill, she decides that she would like to invest in a portfolio that is 60 percent in the S&P 500 and 40 percent in one-month U.S. Treasury Bills. With this in mind, she asks, "What is the expected value after one year, as well as the 95-percent and 68-percent certainty ranges?"

Realizing that you need to do a bit more math (beyond the scope of this book) than just add figures to calculate the combined standard deviation, you make your calculations and come up with the following (Figure 3.5):

- An expected value of $108,300 after one year using a weighted average return of 8.3 percent (an 8.3-percent return of $100,000 yields an end value of $108,300)
- A 95-percent certainty range of $108,300 +/- 2 x $13,800 (based on the combined standard deviation of 13.8 percent, and 0.138 x $100,000 is $13,800)

o   This yields a low value of $80,700 and a high value
    of $135,900
- A 68-percent certainty range of $108,300 +/- $13,800
    o   This yields a certainty range of $94,500 to $122,100

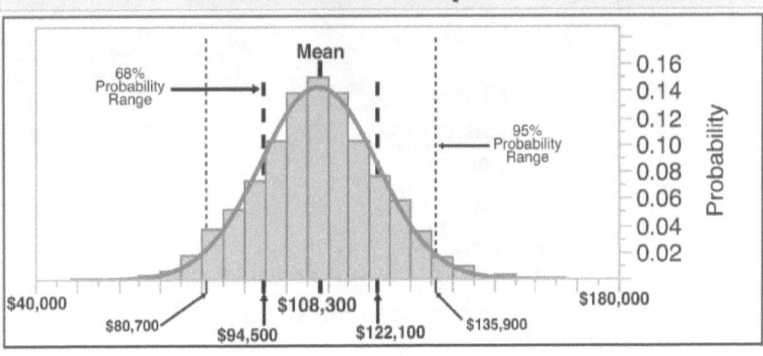

**Figure 3.5**
**Potential Range of Susie's 60/40 Blend**
**Portfolio After One Year**

From looking at the subject figures, the bell curve for the 60/40
diversified portfolio doesn't look much narrower and steeper than
that for the 100-percent S&P 500 portfolio. However, if you look
at the steepness of the peak on each of the curves, you'll see that the
peak of the 60/40 diversified bell curve is steeper and narrower than
for the 100-percent S&P 500 bell curve. Also, the bars on the 60/40
diversified portfolio chart are a bit more orderly than those of the
100 percent S&P 500 portfolio.

What is the difference between the bars and the fitted bell
curves? The bars are from a random number simulation run using
500 trials with the appropriate mean and standard deviation, i.e.,
they're the actual numbers from a simulation vs. the calculation from
an equation, which results in a perfectly smooth bell curve. Can the
difference be significant? Absolutely! (Table 3.4).

| Investment => | S&P 500 | 1 Mo Tbill | 60/40 |
|---|---|---|---|
| Input **Mean** | $ 111,500 | $ 103,453 | $ 108,281 |
| Model Output Mean | $ 111,272 | $ 103,646 | $ 107,714 |
| Difference in Dollars | $ (228) | $ 192 | $ (567) |
| Difference in Percent | -0.2% | 0.2% | -0.5% |
| | | | |
| Input **Std Dev** | $ 17,600 | $ 3,183 | $ 13,780.75 |
| Model Output Std Dev | $ 16,619 | $ 3,033 | $ 13,476 |
| Difference in Dollars | $ (981) | $ (151) | $ (305) |
| Difference in Percent | -5.6% | -4.7% | -2.2% |
| **The Take Away:** | Beware of the limitations of any model you're relying on. | | |

### Table 3.4
### Calculated from Equation vs. Simulated Trial Results

Although one can get smoother bell curve bars by running more simulations, say 10,000 instead of 500, you should keep in mind that you have one chance at the future, not hundreds or thousands. Thus, as you look at the probability ranges, it's critical to keep in mind the limitations of statistical models. You must take some risk to generate enough gain to live off your portfolio; however, the risk/return knife cuts both ways. Fortunately, as mentioned before, through portfolio design, as discussed in Chapter 4, you can do things to bend the risk/reward continuum in your favor.

Are the previous issues discussed by the average financial advisor? Probably not for at least three reasons: First, most brokers and advisors don't understand or have the basic statistical skills necessary to explain the above, even those with lots of letters like CFP, MBA, etc. behind their name. Second, most brokers and advisors are probably not aware of the figures. And third, regrettably, most brokers and advisors are probably afraid of losing the client if the client learned the actual figures. As a whole, it's a case of ignorance is bliss for both sides – until reality strikes – which happens, sooner or later.

## An Example from 2008–2010

Another example of the risk/return continuum in action can be taken from the 2008–2010 performance data of several different asset classes. The financial crisis of 2008 was the worst calendar year for equity markets since the Great Depression, followed by a rebound in 2009 and 2010. The data is from funds managed with a similar efficient market/three-factor-model strategy but in different asset classes.

Returns for 2008 ranged per the following:

- A 54.5-percent loss for the Dimensional Fund Advisors (DFA) Emerging Market Small Cap Portfolio[5]
- A 44.0-percent loss for the DFA International Core Equity Portfolio[6]
- A 36.9-percent loss for the DFA U.S. Core Equity 2 Portfolio[7]
- A 4.0-percent gain for the DFA Five-Year Global Fixed Income Portfolio[8]

For 2009–10 the returns for the same funds were:

- Gains of 99.7 percent and 30.2 percent, respectively, for the DFA Emerging Market Small Cap Portfolio.
- Gains of 39.3 percent and 13.9 percent, respectively, for the DFA International Core Equity Portfolio.
- Gains of 29.2 percent and 21.8 percent, respectively, for the DFA U.S. Core Equity Portfolio.
- Gains of 4.2 percent and 5.3 percent, respectively, for the DFA Five-Year Global Fixed Income Portfolio.

Figure 3.6 shows both the returns in a table as well as a bar/column chart:

## Annual Returns by Year for Different Asset Classes

| Fund | Return for 2008 | Return for 2009 | Return for 2010 |
|------|------|------|------|
| DFA Emerging Markets Small Cap | -54.5% | 99.7% | 30.2% |
| DFA International Core Equity | -44.0% | 39.3% | 13.9% |
| DFA U.S. Core Equity 2 | -36.9% | 29.2% | 21.8% |
| DFA Five-Year Global Fixed Income | 4.0% | 4.2% | 5.3% |

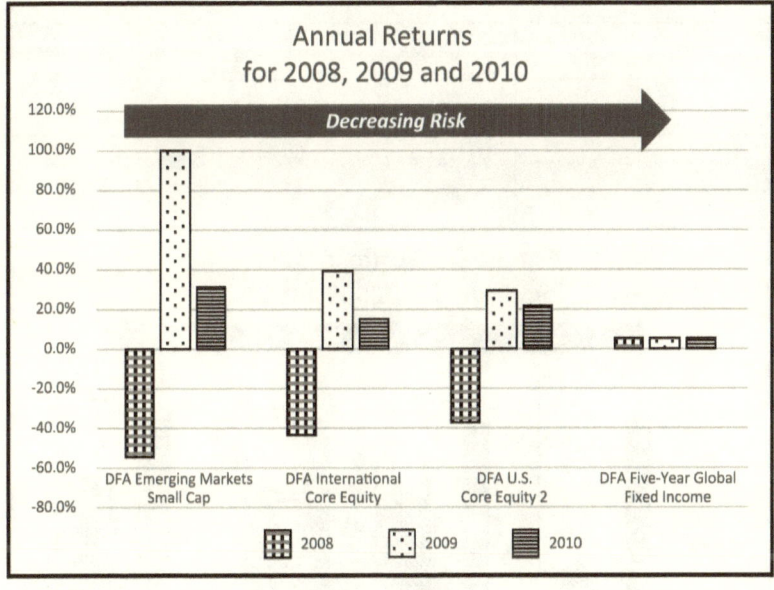

### Figure 3.6
### 2008-10 Return Performance for Various Risk Investments
*Past performance does not predict future performance*

Looking at the three-year trek of a $100,000 investment in each of the subject funds on January 1, 2008, using only their total for each year, makes the point even more tangible (Figure 3.7). Specifically, the value of a $100,000 investment at the close of trading on December 31, 2007, would be, at the close of trading on December 31, 2010:

- $118,304 for the DFA Emerging Market Small Cap Portfolio
- $88,851 for the DFA International Core Equity Portfolio
- $99,298 for the DFA U.S. Core Equity 2 Portfolio
- $114,112 for the DFA Five-Year Global Fixed Income Portfolio

## Portfolio Value by Year for Different Asset Classes

| Fund | Investment on Dec 31, 2007 | Value on Dec 31, 2008 | Value on Dec 31, 2009 | Value on Dec 31, 2010 |
|---|---|---|---|---|
| DFA Emerging Markets Small Cap | $ 100,000 | $ 45,500 | $ 90,864 | $ 118,304 |
| DFA International Core Equity | $ 100,000 | $ 56,000 | $ 78,008 | $ 88,851 |
| DFA U.S. Core Equity 2 | $ 100,000 | $ 63,100 | $ 81,525 | $ 99,298 |
| DFA Five-Year Global Fixed Income | $ 100,000 | $ 104,000 | $ 108,368 | $ 114,112 |

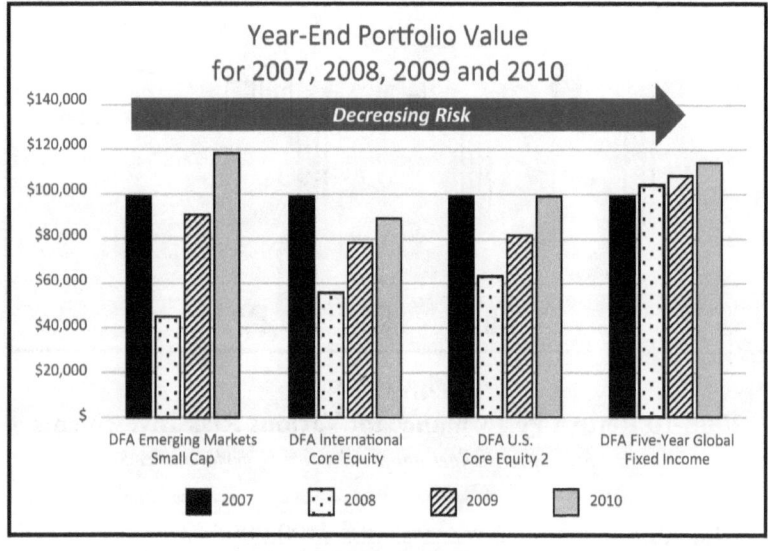

**Figure 3.7**
**2008-10 Financial Performance for Various Risk Investments**
*Past performance does not predict future performance*

Hence, the link between risk and reward is clear. To be sure, the results will have inherent statistical uncertainty. Moreover, imperfections do exist, such as international-developed market equities having a higher risk and lower return than domestic U.S. equities. Nevertheless, the example using actual figures shows that risk and reward are related, and volatility increases with risk.

## The Impact of Time on Risk and Return

Up to this point we've discussed risk and return using short-term time horizons. What happens to risk as we extend the investment time horizon? The answer is encouraging.

For the sake of comparison and discussion, we'll look at the return of three different investments: U.S. Short-Term Treasury Bills; U.S. Long-Term Government Bonds; and the S&P 500 Index. Further, we'll evaluate both total, or nominal, returns, as well as inflation-adjusted ("real") returns. And finally, we'll look at returns over one-, five- and 10-year periods. The data will be from January 1, 1930 through December 31, 2015.

This time horizon was chosen because the U.S. stock market was largely unregulated and thus a bit haphazard before the crash of 1929. More specifically, prior to 1929, securities lacked accounting standards, trading rules and countless other basic standards.

Analyzing the information, we have:

- 86 one-year time periods
- 82 five-year time periods
- 77 ten-year time periods

In summary, without taking inflation into account, the likelihood of ending with more money than you started increases substantially for all three investment options (Figure 3.8, which contains both a table and a bar chart of the data).

## TOTAL Returns (NOT Adjusted for Inflation)
### Chance of Being NEGATIVE Between 1930 and 2015

| | Investment Time Horizon | | |
| --- | --- | --- | --- |
| | 1 Yr | 5 Yr | 10 Yr |
| 1 Month Treasury Bills | 0% | 0% | 0% |
| Long Term Government Bonds | 28% | 5% | 0% |
| S&P 500 | 26% | 11% | 4% |

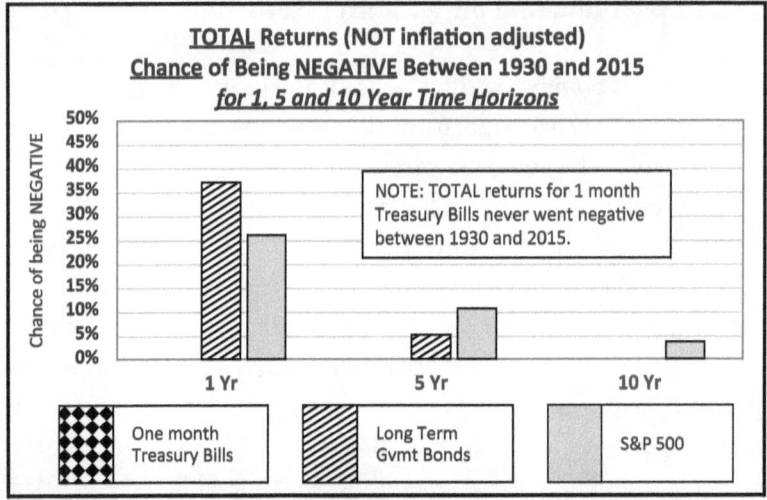

**Figure 3.8**
**TOTAL-Return Chance of Being Negative
with an Increasing Time Horizon**
*Past performance does not predict future performance*

This is easy to understand. In the cases of the treasury bills and long-term government bonds, interest keeps getting deposited into the account so that, over time, even if interest rate changes decrease the value of the bills/bonds, enough interest is earned to finish "ahead"—without taking inflation into account.

In the case of the S&P 500 investment vs. time, we have an investment that grows approximately 11 percent every year while having a one-year standard deviation of approximately 17 percent.

Thus, in time, the total of the returns eventually overrides potential short-term losses resulting from the bumpiness of the standard deviation.

However, to fully model the situation, one needs to incorporate inflation for the *real-return* case. This is where things get interesting.

Like the non-inflation-adjusted *total-return* case, the chance of ending up behind when investing in the S&P 500 decreases with an increasing time frame (Figure 3.9, which again contains both a table and bar chart of the data).

But this is not the case with one month treasury bills or long term government bonds. When factoring inflation into the model, the likelihood of ending up *behind* when holding bills or bonds stays relatively constant at approximately 40 percent. This is eye-opening: ***An investor who holds either a short-, intermediate- or long-term position in U.S. Government Bonds has a 35-percent to 40-percent chance of not keeping up with inflation.*** Moreover, the real return gain, when positive, will be small.

**REAL Returns (Adjusted for Inflation)**
Chance of Being **NEGATIVE** Between 1930 and 2015

|  | Investment Time Horizon | | |
|---|---|---|---|
|  | 1 Yr | 5 Yr | 10 Yr |
| 1 Month Treasury Bills | 42% | 41% | 43% |
| Long Term Government Bonds | 41% | 38% | 43% |
| S&P 500 | 31% | 23% | 13% |

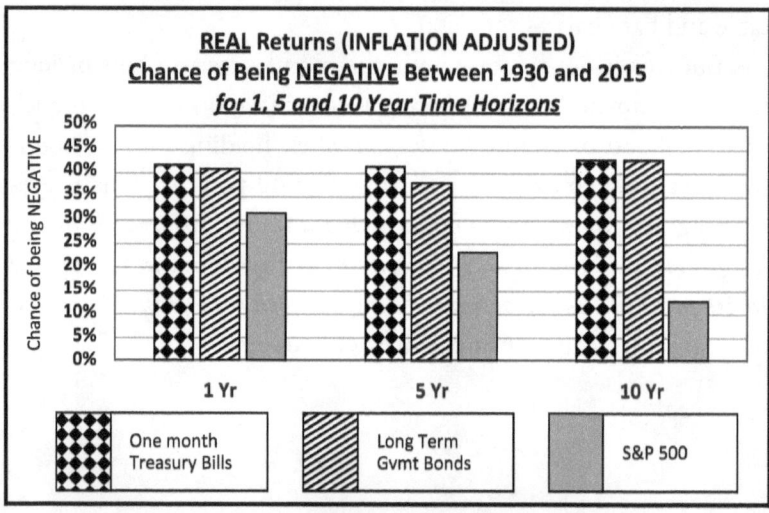

**Figure 3.9**
**REAL-Return Chance of Being Negative**
**with an Increasing Time Horizon**
*Past performance does not predict future performance*

From this, one may immediately, and somewhat erroneously, jump to the conclusion that over a medium to long period, when factoring in inflation, there is a lower risk in holding the S&P 500 than in holding U.S. Treasury Bills or U.S. Long-Term Government Bonds. However, one must remember that the stocks gain and lose far more than treasury bills or bonds because the standard deviation/ variability of stocks is far more than that of the bills or bonds. It's not as simple as looking at whether you gain or lose. You also must look at the potential size of a gain or loss and whether you will end up positive or negative over the relevant time horizon.

Looking at the growth of $1 over the 1926–2015 time frame further illustrates the difference in holding stocks vs. bills or bonds. Although the past does not predict the future, it's interesting to see that $1 invested in the S&P 500 in 1926 would have grown to an inflation-adjusted value of $408 in 2015 (Figure 3.10). In comparison, $1 invested in U.S. One-Month Treasury Bills or U.S. Long-Term Government Bonds would have grown to $1.56 and $10, respectively. One can see that over this 86-year period, the difference is stark.

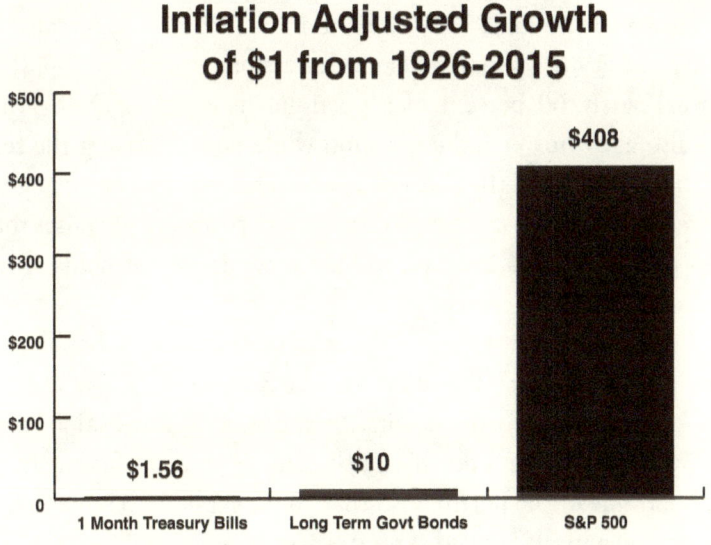

**Figure 3.10**
**1926-2015 Inflation Adjusted Growth of $1**
*Past performance does not predict future performance*

In short, if one wants to increase real (inflation-adjusted) capital by investing in the security markets, one needs to have a significant equity holding. Holding U.S. Treasury Bills and/or U.S. Government Bonds yields a 35-percent to 40-percent chance of not staying ahead of inflation.

Further, if one wants to take significant real distributions from a portfolio (say, 2 percent to 3 percent per year over inflation), it is likely that the real, inflation-adjusted value of a bill or bond portfolio will decrease over time. By taking a significant distribution (more than about 1.5 percent of the underlying value) from a U.S. bill/bond portfolio, one is moving toward a gradual, but certain, long-term decline in the portfolio's real value.

In comparison, by applying the strategies and tactics outlined in this book (more specifics in later chapters) one can take an approximately 4+ percent distribution from a portfolio for perpetuity—if holding a reasonable equity position—while also giving oneself periodic raises for inflation. What is "a reasonable equity position"? For general discussion purposes, holding approximately 60 percent of a portfolio in equities. Doing this will also allow for periodic inflation while not decreasing the real purchasing power of the invested funds. This is a key financial goal of every retiree: To live off his investment portfolio, to get raises that keep pace with inflation, and to have a portfolio that holds semi-steady in real dollar terms.

From this you may ask: "What is the purpose of bonds and why hold any at all?" The short answer is that bonds play at least two key roles in a portfolio. First, if you need a distribution from the portfolio during a down equity market, you can take it from the bond side of the portfolio so that you don't have to sell equities during down markets. And second, an appropriate holding of high-quality, short- to intermediate-term bonds will dampen the portfolio volatility sufficiently to keep it within your risk tolerance. One of the worst things you can do is to venture outside of your risk tolerance and then sell during a down market.

Further on this point, human emotions tend to lead investors to buy high and sell low, a practice that will undermine a portfolio. Also, because no one is clairvoyant and because security prices follow a random walk model, trying to time market highs and lows is futile.

Thus, the best solution is to follow a long-term, calculated, guided and consistent strategy that stays within your risk tolerance.

## The Reality Concerning Investment Return Bell Curves

Up to this point, for simplicity, we've been using symmetrical bell curves with a "normal" distribution; i.e., the left and right sides of the bell curve mirror each other. However, in reality, the bell curves for investments skew to the right (Figure 3.11).

## Log Normal Distribution

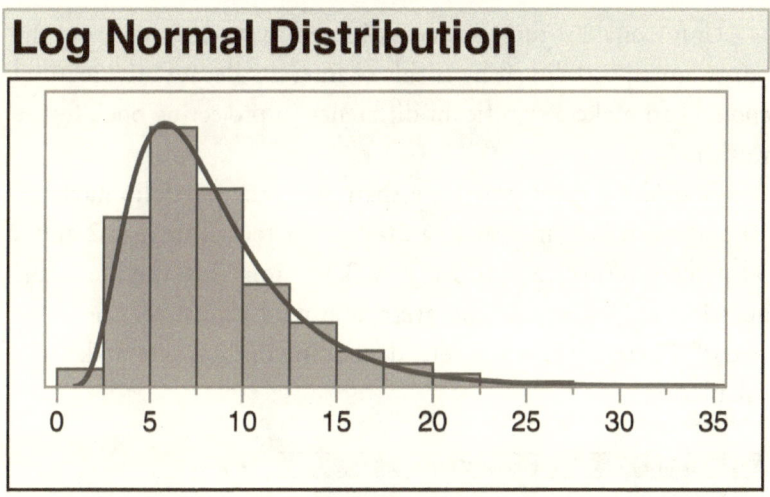

**Figure 3.11**
**An Example of a "Skewed to the Right" Distribution**

Why is this so? It's simple: The worst one can do with an unleveraged, publicly traded investment (one in which no money was borrowed to buy the security and there is no legal risk to holding the investment) is to lose everything. But in theory, the investment can make a nearly infinite return. Hence, investments have bell curves that are "skewed to the right."

Skewed bell curves have different equations for calculating probability ranges, and sophisticated investment software will take this into account. But for simplicity, I've focused on *normal* (symmetrical) bell curves. Once one understands normal bell curves and uncertainty, it's easy to get software and estimates that more closely resemble the real world. Nevertheless, for discussion and understanding purposes, normal bell curves are more than adequate to start understanding the situation and applying the information.

## A Brief Note on Arithmetic Return vs. Geometric Return

Unfortunately, there are two different ways of calculating the return on a portfolio. Why is this of interest? Because the method chosen can make a significant difference in projecting one's future wealth.

Consider a three-year time span, with the portfolio having a 10-percent return in year 1, a 20-percent return in year 2 and a 30-percent return in year 3 (Table 3.5). From this, the inevitable question is "What was the average annual return for the three years?" There are two answers, depending on how one makes the calculation.

| Year | Return | Arithmetic Average | Geometric Average |
|------|--------|--------------------|--------------------|
| 1 | 10% | Return = 1/3 x (1.10+1.20+1.30) | Return = (1.10x1.20x1.30) |
| 2 | 20% | = 1/3x(3.60) | = (1.7160) |
| 3 | 30% | = 1.20 | = 1.1972 |
| | | Average Return = 20.00% | Average Return = 19.72% |
| | | *Note the significant difference in the returns calculated above. Over a multi-year time period the difference can be substantial.* | |

### Table 3.5
### Arithmetic vs. Geometric Return

Although the difference may look subtle, it can be significant when factored over many years with widely swinging (high standard deviation) returns such as those likely with stocks/equities. The greater the number of years and the wider the swings, the bigger the difference between the arithmetic and geometric average return.

Which is right? Without getting into the minutia, each is right and wrong in its own way. Engineers and others with strong quantitative skills are particularly vulnerable to the discrepancy because they often make the calculations without being aware of the subtle but significant difference.

## Converting Your Risk Tolerance to Standard Deviation

At this point you may be thinking: "All this standard deviation and bell curve stuff is fine, but how do I convert my personal risk tolerance to a standard deviation and bell curve?" That's a good and logical question.

Fortunately, good portfolio analysis and optimization software has something called a *risk tolerance* questionnaire. By combining your answers to questions about how you would behave under different market transitions and your investment time horizon, the software can calculate a standard deviation that fits your personal risk tolerance and time horizon.

Why is your time horizon a part of the equation? Because as you get closer to the point of making withdrawals (retirement), you need to reduce the standard deviation/uncertainty/risk of the portfolio because you have less time to recover from downward price movements. Remember, free and open markets follow a random-walk model and even "blue chip" stocks can be volatile.

You can find risk tolerance questionnaires all over the internet, but they generally give vague answers such as: "You're a moderate-risk investor" or "you're an aggressive investor." You need more than this, as you need a risk tolerance questionnaire that converts your answers to the appropriate standard deviation, or range of standard deviations.

However, even with this it's still just a questionnaire. The real test is when you're in the middle of a bear market. That's the time to speak with your financial advisor about your feelings on risk tolerance. A good advisor will ask you about this, or at least communicate with you, during bear markets as well as bull markets, to better gauge your personal risk tolerance. Moreover, a good advisor can, through time and conversations, gauge your risk tolerance so that you're ready for the inevitable bear markets when they arrive.

## A Shortcoming of Standard Deviation as Risk

To be sure, measuring all aspects of risk is not as simple as measuring the standard deviation. For example, if one had an investment that lost exactly 10 percent per year for 29 years, the investment would have lost 95.3 percent of its value while having a standard deviation of zero. This is because standard deviation is a measure of how much the set of numbers vary. In this case, the annual loss didn't vary, so its standard deviation would be zero. Nevertheless, the risk is significant because the loss is significant.

What are you to do? Keep in mind that numbers and statistics are very good tools, but you still need to know their limitations.

Going back to this hypothetical investment that lost exactly 10 percent a year for 29 years, how many companies would stay in business and keep their management structure together if they consistently lost 10 percent a year? Probably none. Hence, by applying a bit of common sense on both sides of the equation, we can see that standard deviation is a good, readily available proxy for measuring risk. It's not perfect, but it's a good start.

## A Word About Value and Growth

As mentioned above, one needs to temper the math and statistics with good judgment. Evaluating value stocks vs. growth stocks is an example.

Value stocks, as discussed in Chapter 2, are those that have a high asset value to stock price. This is because the company appears to be having trouble, or is in a troubled industry, and the market has thus beat down the stock price to the point that it has a low stock-to-asset value. Inversely, one could also say that a value stock has a high asset value compared with its stock price value. Because the stock price has been beaten down, one would expect it to be riskier.

Taking this to the next logical step, one would expect large-cap (big company) value stocks to have a higher standard deviation than large-cap growth stocks. This seems logical, as value stocks, by subjective analysis, are riskier and thus have a higher expected return than growth stocks.

However, the data indicates this is not the case. Large-cap value stocks have a lower standard deviation than large-cap growth stocks. Should one thus conclude that value stocks are lower risk than growth stocks? No.

What is happening? One can offer endless thoughts on the subject, but from my simple viewpoint, growth stocks are sitting on a higher price-to-earnings perch than the value stocks, giving them more room to fall and thus giving them a higher standard deviation. I haven't seen research supporting this, but it's one explanation that I can offer. And for an explanation of why growth stocks have a higher price-to-asset value than value stocks, one can argue that the market expects growth stocks to grow more and/or faster than value stocks as a reflection of their higher price relative to assets.

## Summary

Risk is a real part of any investment equation. To invest successfully, you need to understand the amount of risk you are taking and deal with it appropriately. Fortunately, some fairly elementary, easy to understand statistical methods can be applied to determine and manage the risk of your portfolio.

Statistics is not a case of sadistics; rather it's something you can use to your advantage. Using uncertainty as a definition of risk facilitates the quantification of your risk so that you can know the expected dollar impact. Further, what's presented in this book can put you in a position that's analogous to making a living as a casino owner instead of a casino gambler. In short, elementary statistics can turn a headwind into a tailwind while also giving you an estimate of how rough the ride will be.

Bell curves graphically portray an investment's risk. Do you know what the bell curve of your investment portfolio looks like? This is an answer you should know if you want to invest responsibly. Your bell curve will tell you about what kind of return to expect, over the long term, and how much volatility, or heartburn, you'll need to endure to get that return.

From what you know to this point, do you think there's an optimal way to mix the various investment options to get the best possible risk/return ratio? In the next chapter we'll again take an analogy from another subject as we want to make investing simple, fun and profitable. Again, the objective is to raise your return, reduce your risk and cut your cost. This will benefit other aspects of your life immeasurably.

---

1.  Pfaffenberger and Patterson, *Statistical Methods for Business and Economics*, inside cover, Irwin, 1987.
2.  © 2018, Morningstar, Inc. All Rights Reserved. The information contained herein: (1) is proprietary to Morningstar and/or its content providers; (2) may not be copied or distributed; (3) does not constitute investment advice offered by Morningstar; and (4) is not warranted to be accurate, complete or timely. Neither Morningstar nor its content providers are responsible for any damages or losses arising from any use of this information. Past performance is no guarantee of future results. Use of information from Morningstar does not necessarily constitute agreement by Morningstar, Inc. of any investment philosophy or strategy presented in this publication.

3. www.pages.stern.nyu.edu, spring 2018 (since changed)
4. www.seekingalpha.com, spring 2018 (since changed)
5. 2017 prospectus for the DFA Emerging Market Small Cap Portfolio.
6. 2017 prospectus for the DFA International Core Equity Portfolio.
7. 2017 prospectus for the DFA U.S. Core Equity 2 Portfolio.
8. 2017 prospectus for the DFA Five-Year Global Fixed Income Portfolio.

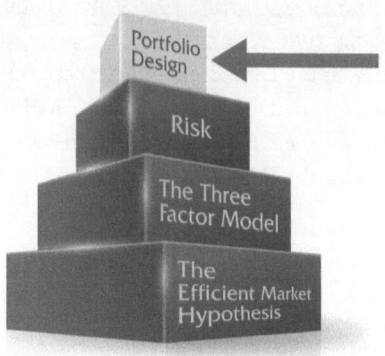

## CHAPTER 4

# Diversification

**Unconventional Wisdom**
*Diversification, done scientifically and correctly, is far more than "not putting all your eggs in one basket". Your portfolio, just like a chef's dinner, has the potential to be significantly more than the sum of its parts. How? There's a reason Harry Markowitz won a Nobel Prize in 1992 for figuring this out in the 1950s. And although it's Nobel Prize winning stuff, we'll make it easy to understand. Read on; as it's ingenious!*

Would you like a simple yet solid understanding of how to get the most possible return for the amount of risk you're willing to take? A key piece to answering this question is portfolio diversification, combined with what we've learned from Chapters 1–3.

Portfolio diversification is a highly misunderstood subject concerning personal investing. Investors commonly think that diversification is simply "not putting all your eggs in one basket."

While this is part of the equation, it is far from all that one needs to know to invest optimally.

Fortunately, as with the subjects covered in the previous chapters, we can use a simple analogy to explain what is happening.


## Investing Compared to a Chef in the Kitchen

Do you think a master chef randomly mixes ingredients to create a masterpiece? Definitely not. Each ingredient has a specific purpose, and the end product is far greater than the sum of each ingredient taken individually. To better understand portfolio diversification, we'll first take a tangible example from the kitchen.

Option 1: Living on Flour Alone. If you were to go into a kitchen and pull out one ingredient, flour, it would keep you from starving. Yes, you may become a bit malnourished and yes, it may taste terrible. However, if you were hungry enough the flour would be tolerable and you would eat it to keep from starving.

This is analogous to having a portfolio with only one asset. Maybe the asset is ExxonMobil stock, or maybe it's bonds from the Kansas City Municipal Water District. You may not go broke, but you're far from experiencing all the potential benefits of a diversified global economy.

This may sound a bit absurd, but you'd be surprised how often it occurs. How? It's easy. An investor with an employer-provided 401(k) plan faces many unknown investments vs. one he knows something about, his employer's stock. So that's what he often chooses. It's probably better than nothing, but it's far from optimal.

Among other possible shortcomings, this investor is doubling down on individual risk. How? The employer's signature is on this investor's paycheck as well as the company's stock. If the employer hits hard times, the investor's stock will go down and he may concurrently lose his job.

Sadly, this is a common situation. I've seen far too many cases of the once high-flying and/or "stable" company that encounters difficult times while the employee-investor loses a job and a substantial part of his net worth. The company doesn't usually go bankrupt, but 10 years after the company started its gradual slide into mediocrity the employee-investor finds himself unemployed with most of his net worth in a stock that hasn't increased in value for 10 years.

Having a portfolio composed largely of a single stock, whether it's one's employer's or not, is somewhat like people in rural China who have lived for millennia on a diet that overwhelmingly consists of rice. They can survive on it, but there is significant room for improvement.

Option 2: Many Random Ingredients. The next option is to consider a well-stocked, modern kitchen and pantry, but having a cook who randomly throws things together. Hence, you end up with a bowl that has random amounts of ketchup, vanilla, flour, sugar, chocolate, hamburger meat, crumbled blue cheese, salt, salami, chicken, carrots, garlic and maybe even a little salmon. The cook then bakes it for a random amount of time at a random temperature before serving the result. Yuk!

But, once again, if you're hungry enough you'll eat it to keep from starving. And this time, unlike the flour only offering of Option 1, you won't have to worry about being malnourished. It may taste hideous, maybe even worse than the flour-only diet, but you'll get a "diversified" blend of foods with a variety of vitamins, fiber and protein.

Surprisingly, this is an approach that many investors take to their portfolio. They look at the range of offerings, particularly in the case of investing 401(k) assets, and randomly pick from the options, largely based on the packaging; i.e., the marketing driven name of the mutual fund. Adding to the dysfunction is the fact that many of the investments may be overlapping. Therefore, while the investor may think they're diversifying their portfolio, they're just purchasing the same ingredients in different packaging.

Next, just like baking the random kitchen concoction for a random amount of time, the investor randomly moves in and out of the various investments based on the moment's whim. Or, more likely, he buys and sells the various investments based on what he heard from last night's pundit of the hour, his neighbor, his brother-in-law or some other random opinion.

With the ingredients of random opinions, emotion, "gut instinct," a variety of ingredients and well-intended buys and sells, the result is far from optimal. Even worse, since the decisions are not based on relevant factual analysis, it's a recipe for disaster, no pun intended. The result is an investor crossing the finish line to retirement with a fraction of what he could have had for the same amount of money invested.

Option 3: Add Some Study and Common Sense. Going back to the kitchen analogy, in this case the cook has become literate and picked up a cook book. Wow! The diner finds that the outcome can be a pleasant, nutritious experience. To be sure, it takes more work and care than a one-ingredient diet or a randomly generated meal, but the result is worth the extra effort.

Similar to the kitchen experience, the investor in this situation can obtain a good result. Based on science and statistics, the investor mixes the specified ingredients in the specified proportions, gives it the right amount of time to grow with sufficient incoming funds, and presto, he retires with a significant nest egg. It took some work and required a few risks (the raw egg didn't look too good going into the bowl), but the outcome justified everything that went into it.

However, just as a well-stocked kitchen contains plenty of "junk" food ingredients and foodstuffs with additives we'd rather not think about, the world of investment options contains many "junk" investment options and harmful ingredients. Just as she needs to be cognizant of what's in the food she eats, the investor needs to be responsible about what goes into her portfolio.

Unfortunately, just as a high proportion of what's sold in an average grocery store is not good for the purchaser, a high proportion of what's commonly sold in the investment world is not good for the investor. The "junk" isles of a grocery store may be better than eating flour alone or trying to force down a randomly mixed dish, but it's far less healthy than using all fresh ingredients with the perfect mix of seasonings.

Option 4: Enter the Master Chef. Once again going to the well-stocked kitchen and pantry, this time you bring in a formally trained, highly experienced master chef. Then, using common ingredients that came from the local grocery store (mostly fresh and with minimal additives), he creates a masterpiece meal. And in addition to tasting great, it's very nutritious and balanced. It even looks good when the chef puts it on the plate. That's what we want!

In the world of investing, our master chef is a Nobel Prize winner named Harry Markowitz, who is known in investing circles as "the father of modern portfolio theory." But unlike employing a master chef, using the investment principles developed by Harry Markowitz doesn't cost a premium. Conversely, the best ingredients often cost less than the lower quality ingredients, kind of like the fresh foods in a grocery store often cost less than all the junk and prepared food.

Do you remember the index funds we discussed in Chapter 1? They're a very good ingredient for a well-designed portfolio built for maximum return per unit of risk and unit of cost. Further, you can go beyond index funds to something better, more refined and better performing per unit of risk than even index funds. These investment options are something I'll describe as "asset based market funds," and I'll discuss them in Chapter 5.

Option 5: Get the Customized Taste You Desire. Although the meal has gotten exponentially better and more nutritious than just flour and water, you can still take it one step further by having the master chef prepare the meal of your choice, seasoned to your personal desire and cooked to your liking using his skills and the available ingredients. This is the ideal meal, and one that has an analogy in portfolio design. By applying the findings of Harry Markowitz, especially if combined with what's presented in Chapters 1-3, you can develop an optimal portfolio that's tailored to your risk tolerance and time horizon but still uses the available ingredients.

Notice that the meal, like the portfolio, is made with "the available ingredients." You don't have to use index funds or asset-based market funds to significantly improve your portfolio. Yes, it does take an array of ingredients, but just as a master chef doesn't have to exclusively use Class A optimal ingredients to make a great meal, you can usually make a very good portfolio with the funds available in your 401(k). And if you're investing outside of your 401(k), the world is your pantry.

## Scientific Diversification, In Simple Terms

Modern portfolio optimization started back in the early 1950s when the young Markowitz entered the economics PhD program at The University of Chicago, the same place that later minted Eugene Fama and the efficient market hypothesis. Harry must have been a very bright and promising student, as he was assigned to work for his doctoral dissertation under Milton Friedman, a star in economic circles who would win the Nobel Prize in economics in 1976.

While Markowitz was still considering research topics for his doctoral thesis, one day a stock broker suggested that he do something concerning stocks and the market[1]. Ultimately, Markowitz decided to research risk and return for various investment options.

Although stock market and investment options are heavily researched at today's top academic institutions, it was a bit unusual to do so at a highly respected university in the early 1950s. PhD candidates in economics departments commonly worked on classical economic research, as common stocks and the markets were not considered worthy of serious academic focus. However, what Markowitz discovered not only earned him his PhD, it built his pre-eminent status in portfolio theory and ultimately earned him the Nobel Prize in economics (some 40 years later, in 1992).

To understand what Markowitz discovered, consider the stocks for two companies, Smith and Jones. Each company has a risk (standard deviation) and an expected return, with Jones having a higher risk and expected return than Smith (Figure 4.1). If you were to construct a portfolio composed of Smith and Jones, you'd logically expect the combined risk and return to lie somewhere on a straight line connecting the two companies. The assumption is both linear and logical.

However, by applying the mathematical tools of statistical covariance and linear programming, Markowitz discovered that a combination of Smith and Jones could lie upward and to the left of the straight line connecting them (Figure 4.2). This was brilliant. It was groundbreaking!

Why? He found that one can potentially get more return for the same amount of risk, or the same return for less risk. This is the core of what the investor wants: more return, less risk.

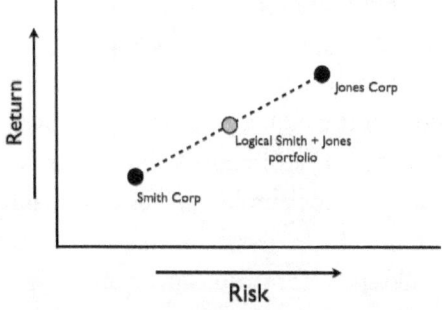

**Figure 4.1**
**Logical Smith + Jones Risk/Return**

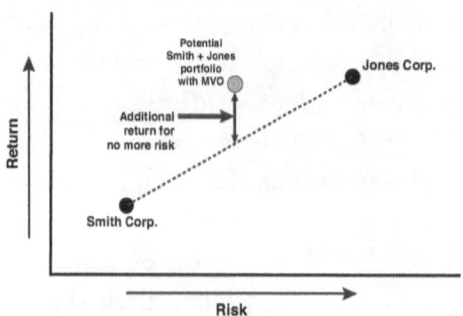

**Figure 4.2**
**Potential Smith + Jones Risk/Return**

If you consider all the possible investments in the world, both stocks and bonds (and other things as well), and their infinite number of possible combinations, you would get something resembling half of an egg lying on its side (Figure 4.3). This is interesting, as it indicates that one can find optimal combinations of prospective investments that lie as far up and to the left as possible. Points along this curve represent what's known in investment parlance as *the efficient frontier*, the point where one gets the greatest possible expected return per unit of risk.

In summary, Markowitz's work revealed two important things. First, a scientifically diversified portfolio will outperform an undiversified portfolio. And second, by applying the appropriate mathematical tools, one can design the optimum portfolio for a given amount of risk.

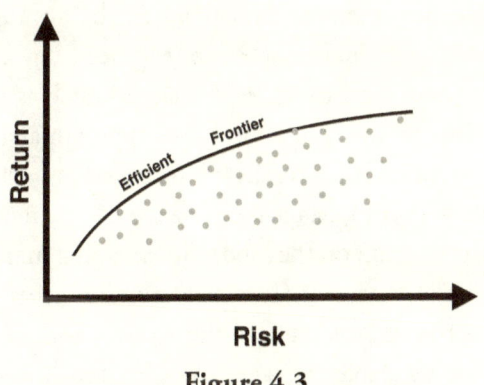

**Figure 4.3**
**The Efficient Frontier**

## A Shortcoming of the Efficient Frontier

While mean variance optimization (MVO)—the essence of Markowitz's work—is a very good tool to apply to one's portfolio, it is not a panacea for determining the optimal investment mix. At its root, MVO is a mathematical solution applied to an economic/

investment finance problem. What does this mean? One must be skillful and cautious in applying it.

For example, if you were to buy a commercially available MVO tool that is powered by Markowitz's math and fed by expected returns and standard deviations of common investments (large, small, domestic, international and emerging-market stocks and a mix of bonds), you could get some answers that don't make common sense. Say you were to enter a risk tolerance of 16 percent (standard deviation) and let the model run without constraints. You could get an optimal recommended portfolio of 35 percent cash and 65 percent emerging-market stocks. That's alarming! Would a prudent investor put his life savings in a portfolio that is 65 percent emerging market stocks? This clearly would not represent the global economy.

What's happening? The MVO model is giving its best mathematical solution without regard for the global economy and common sense. It's a mathematical model being applied to an economic/investment finance question (engineers beware).

What does one need to do in this situation? It is necessary to apply constraints to the model. Because approximately 5 percent to 10 percent of the world's total capital market is in the emerging markets (Turkey, Poland, Malaysia, Brazil, etc.), the model operator needs to put a constraint on the model for emerging markets, such as a portfolio limit of 5 percent. The exact number depends on many things, such as the risk tolerance of the investor and the investment options that are available. However, the bottom line is the same, as one needs to put a well-reasoned constraint on the emerging-market percentage. Good MVO software will allow the user to add reasonable constraints.

Putting constraints on the MVO model causes the efficient frontier curve to shift downward and to the right. While that's the opposite direction in which we would like to go, if the constraints imposed are reasonable, the investor will be better off. Many company 401(k) plans have somewhat restricted investment options, so one may have to apply some constraints to make the optimal portfolio conform to what's available.

This brings up another point, and that concerns the person running the MVO model. To be sure, anyone can purchase an MVO model and apply it to a portfolio. However, unless you are experienced with linear programming, statistical covariance, mathematical models and global financial markets, it's probably best to hire someone with the skill set to run the model and generate the optimal investment mix.

This isn't a carte blanche recommendation for financial advisors, as the overwhelming majority of them do not have the skill set necessary to prudently run an MVO model. So you need to be careful about whom you select, how the model is run and how its findings are applied.

## A Word About Bonds

Bonds come in all different shapes and sizes. However, the two key base features of a bond are:

1) Its **quality,** i.e., how probable the bond is to return its full obligation to the investor and not default on the payment of either interest or principal. The lower the quality, the higher the risk and the higher the interest rate the bond will need to pay.

2) Its **duration,** or the amount of time that expires before the principal is due back to the investor. The longer the duration, the greater the risk and generally the higher the interest rate the bond will need to pay. Generally, short-term bond interest rates are lower than long-term bond interest rates. For this discussion, we will assume that we are not in the unusual situation of an *inverted yield curve*, which is when short term rates are higher than long term rates.

From this, you may immediately think: "Because I want the highest possible interest, I want low-quality, long-term bonds." However, the core reasons for having a bond position are to:

1) Protect your principal
2) Diversify your portfolio
3) Reduce your portfolio volatility

Therefore, while higher interest payments may be attractive, you shouldn't lose sight of why you should hold bonds in the first place. Hence, when a typical investor is purchasing bonds, he wants to stay with investment-grade, short- to intermediate-term bonds because lower grade bonds can vary in value with changes in equity markets and, thus, somewhat dampen the benefits of diversifying with bonds.

What defines an "investment grade bond"? For corporate bonds, investment grade bonds will have a Baa3 or better rating from Moody's and/or a BBB- or better rating from S&P. Also, when buying corporate bonds, it's good to add a dose of common sense regarding the company, the industry and one's diversification among industries.

For government bonds, I tend to disregard the rating agencies when it comes to U.S. debt and avoid it. Why? On something so large and politically loaded as the U.S. government, I don't trust the ratings agencies. Further, a $20+ trillion national debt on national income of $4.5 trillion is, at some point, unsustainable (see Addendum I).

Regarding the duration of bonds, I tend to keep the maturity date, the date when all principal is due back from the borrower, at six years or less. Why? Life, and especially corporate or government financial strength, is hard to forecast beyond five years. In the age of the Internet, financial viability can change quickly.

Additionally, bond values decrease when interest rates increase, and the impact is exponentially compounded as the time to maturity lengthens. In other words, it's not good to have a bond paying 3-percent interest when the market rate goes up to 5 percent because rising interest rates reduces the value of a bond. Therefore, keeping in mind the primary purposes of your bond position, it's good to purchase investment-grade bonds with a short- to medium-term duration.

Some investors may remember the "good ol' days of 10-percent interest rates." Actually, this perception is an illusion. Why? When interest rates were 10-percent, inflation was approximately 8 percent. Thus, one's real return was only 2 percent (10 percent - 8 percent = 2 percent). Hence, an investor taking the full 10-percent yield from her bond position was in reality slowly liquidating the purchasing power of her portfolio.

## Thoughts on the Global Allocation

Because we live in an interconnected global economy, it makes sense for one to diversify globally. To be sure, the prices of equities are highly correlated across national boundaries. Nevertheless, each country moves somewhat in its own sphere because of regional and national market forces. Therefore, you will improve your portfolio diversification by holding equities from around the world.

Before tackling the amount to invest in each country, one can benefit by understanding global equities fall into three general buckets:

- U.S.
- Developed country (Japan, Great Britain, Germany, etc.)
- Developing country (South Africa, Brazil, Poland, Thailand, etc.)

One can simplify the process substantially by classifying equities into one of these three categories.

The next question is: "How much should I put into each bucket?" If one had no emotions or biases and all countries had equal political risk, the purely analytical answer would be to invest in each country an amount based on a country's share of the international equities market. This would result in approximately 50 percent being in U.S. equities, 42 percent being developed-country equities and 8 percent being in developing-country equities.

However, we do have emotions and biases, and all countries do not have the same risk. Hence, a more reasonable regional breakdown would be 55 percent to 70 percent U.S. equities, 20 percent to 35 percent developed-country equities and 4 percent to 10 percent developing-country equities.

Keep in mind that these are percentages of the equity portion of the portfolio. If the portfolio, for example, is 60 percent equities and 40 percent bonds, one would multiply each of the above percentages by 0.6.

## Summary and Going Forward

In summary, an appropriately diversified portfolio will outperform an undiversified portfolio. Moreover, prudent, scientific diversification involves more than simply "not putting all your eggs in one basket."

Just as a master chef can create a meal that's better than the sum of its ingredients, a competent finance professional can generate a portfolio that performs better than the linear sum of its parts. Further, as a master chef can create a meal that's tailored to the diner, a good finance professional, using good financial software and adequate investment options, can deliver an optimal financial portfolio that's tailored to the investor's personal situation.

Although MVO models have their limitations, the tool in the right hands can be applied to optimize a portfolio. From a broader perspective, an appropriately diversified portfolio will increase the investor's return per unit of risk. This is supported not only by Markowitz's Nobel Prize-winning findings, but also from global portfolio performance data. By applying good investment ingredients in the right proportions, you can get the best possible return per unit of risk.

---

1. Interview of Harry Markowitz by Dimensional Fund Advisors (DFA), 2007.

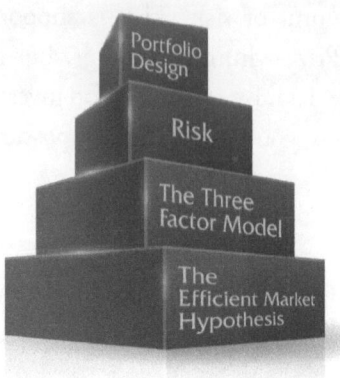

## CHAPTER 5

# Investment Vehicles and Performance Examples

Ideally, the investor would simultaneously apply the principles outlined in Chapters 1–4. However, for a variety of reasons, this may not be possible. Nevertheless, you can make substantial progress without complete adherence to the methods outlined. Following is a brief discussion of the investment vehicle options, followed by a few examples.

## The Investment Vehicle

At the risk of sounding commercially biased, in order of preference for optimal performance the investment vehicle would be:

1) Mutual funds from Dimensional Fund Advisors (DFA)
2) Index funds (Vanguard and others)

3)  Exchange-Traded Funds (ETFs)
4)  Managed/other mutual funds

Keep in mind that neither the publisher nor the author are connected with any investment company or being paid by an investment or mutual fund company.

<u>DFA</u>. Based on noncommercial research, DFA provides the most scientific, cost-effective, performance-driven and market-based mutual funds available at the time of this writing. David Booth and Rex Sinquefield, both PhDs from the University of Chicago, started the company in 1981. Its board members include Eugene Fama and other notable pragmatic researchers. Kenneth French, PhD, Fama's long-time research partner, has worked for DFA many years and contributed significantly to its products and strategies.

As of this writing, DFA, based in Austin, TX, and having approximately 1,200 employees, had $582 billion under management, making it one of the 50 largest money managers in the world. This speaks highly of the company's low cost structure, as $582 billion spread over 1,200 employees averages $485 million managed per employee.

To put this in perspective, ExxonMobil, at the time of this writing, had a market capitalization of $350 billion and 70,000 employees, which equates to $5 million in assets per employee. That makes the asset base per employee at DFA approximately 97 times greater than that of ExxonMobil. Because the two entities serve different industries, this is not a totally fair comparison, but it does illustrate the degree of leverage at DFA.

Moving closer to DFA's industry, financial services, J.P. Morgan Chase, at the time of writing, had $2.5 trillion in assets and 167,000 employees. This equates to almost $15 million in assets per employee. Hence, one can say that each DFA employee manages 32 times more assets than each J.P. Morgan Chase employee.

Taking the comparison one step further, Fidelity Investments, a direct competitor of DFA and one of the world's five largest investment management companies, manages $2.6 trillion with 45,000 employees. This yields an average of $58 million under management per employee, which is approximately one-eighth of the amount managed per employee at DFA.

This book is not about corporate strategy and efficiency. Nevertheless, by adhering to the science described herein, as well as applying numerous strategies beyond the scope of this book, DFA delivers strong market-based returns with costs to the investor that are, on average, approximately 75-percent less than actively managed funds. And by focusing on market science, DFA generally delivers superior returns at a lower cost per unit of risk than other products in each respective class of investments (large stocks, small stocks, bonds, etc.).

To have access to DFA, an investor must either:

A. Be a large institutional investor such as the University of Kansas Endowment Fund or the Boeing Retirement Fund.
B. Get DFA products through a 401(k) plan, if offered.
C. Go through a DFA approved financial advisor

Rather than employ an inefficient army of financial advisors, as do most other companies in the financial services industry, DFA screens advisory companies for philosophical alignment. This gives them control over who offers their products while minimizing payroll and overhead to benefit the investors they serve. The result is a highly efficient investment mechanism for those who can access DFA products.

Index Funds. With assets under management of $5 trillion, Vanguard is the industry pioneer of index funds and another one of the largest money management firms in the world. John Bogle led Vanguard's charge into index funds for many years.

In accordance with the previously discussed corporate efficiency, at the time of this writing Vanguard had 17,000 employees, or $294 million per employee. This is closer to DFA than the aforementioned companies, as it equates to a little more than half the asset level per employee as DFA.

In comparison with the market-based funds of DFA, Vanguard's products are either managed funds or index funds. Unlike DFA, an investor can go directly to Vanguard and invest in its products, which are also commonly offered in 401(k) plans.

While Vanguard's actively managed funds usually have a lower cost than other actively managed funds, they are still more expensive (and likely have higher profit margins for Vanguard) than Vanguard's index funds. Do the higher cost Vanguard actively managed funds get better risk-adjusted returns than their index funds? If they do, Vanguard, at the time of this writing, wasn't making the direct comparison numbers readily available via its website.

While being better at delivering the maximum return per unit of risk than managed funds, index funds merely track a commercial index, such as the S&P 500 or the Russell 2000. Why is this a potential weakness? S&P and other creators of indexes may have created their indexes for something other than optimal market-based investment performance.

Also, an index fund will buy and sell based on the market movement of its index components. While this appears to be what the investor would want, the trades are not always cost-effective; i.e., the cost of the trade may exceed the benefit. In comparison, DFA scientifically incorporates trading costs into its portfolio management to maximize investor return per unit of cost. To be sure, both are winning options, but DFA's products are more scientific than index funds.

ETFs. Exchange traded funds, or ETFs, are, in layman's terms, mutual funds that are packaged as stocks. As such, ETFs trade during the day instead of settling after the market closes, as mutual funds do. Also, one can buy options on ETFs and place limit orders, etc., on ETFs, just as one can do with stocks.

Many, if not most, ETFs are either an index fund or a derivative thereof. For example, in addition to offering securities representing the traditional indexes, such as the S&P 500 and the Russell 2000, security companies also offer products such as "health care index funds" or "oil and gas index funds."

While this may sound like a good idea, one needs to keep in mind that capital flows across industrial boundaries and markets are efficient. Thus, while one specific industry may outperform another from one year to the next, industry is not one of the three factors that explain approximately 90 percent of a portfolio's return. Hence, investing in industry specific ETFs and mutual funds is not advisable.

ETFs versus Index Funds. What about the choice of investing in the S&P 500 through an ETF versus a mutual fund index fund? Although both sides may point to exceptions, for most portfolios it doesn't make a significant difference. It's like the taste difference between Heinz ketchup from a plastic bottle versus Heinz ketchup from a pump-squirt canister at McDonald's. Heinz ketchup is Heinz ketchup. Likewise, an S&P 500 index mutual fund is, from the average investor's perspective, equal to an S&P 500 index ETF.

Managed Funds. In many cases, neither DFA products, nor index funds, nor ETFs are available through an investor's primary investment avenue, which is often their 401(k). However, you can still apply the strategies discussed in Chapters 2–4 to optimize your portfolio and maximize return per unit of risk given your investment options. For example, you can apply the three-factor model from Chapter 2, risk analysis from Chapter 3 and mean-variance optimization from Chapter 4. Doing this will significantly enhance your investment performance and generate a portfolio with an appropriate amount of risk/volatility.

One needs to be aware of potential style drift (fund management tactics that change over time) and other issues, but millions of comfortable, adequate retirement nest eggs have been built using managed funds. Managed funds may not be the most efficient means to the desired destination, but they're often the only investment available. Also, if one has a managed fund investment in a taxable account, the immediate tax hit from selling that position may not be worth the potential gain of moving to an index fund, ETF or a fund from DFA.

## Performance Example 1: Portfolio Growth (Show me the money!)

It would be remiss not to present the growth of a portfolio using the strategies and tactics discussed herein. From the available data, it is evident that portfolio performance supports the points argued in previous chapters (Figures 5.1 and 5.2).

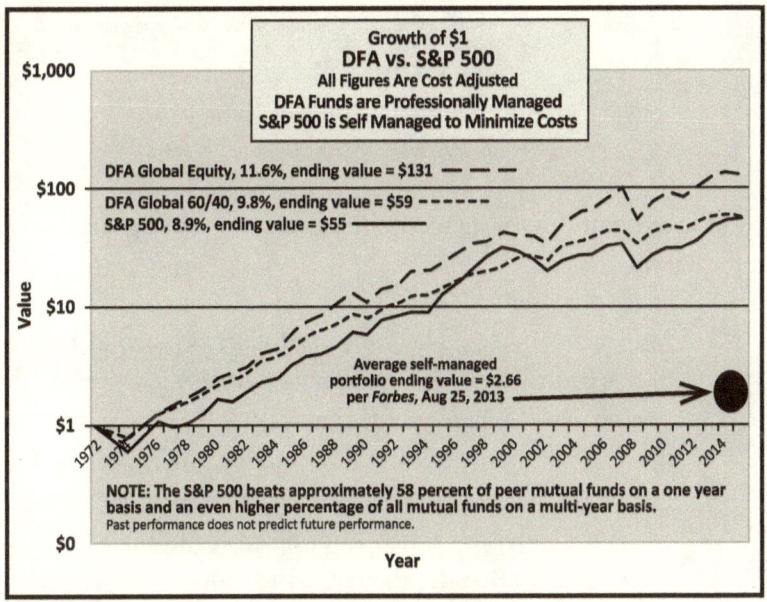

**Figure 5.1**
**Historical Portfolio Performance**[1,2,3,4]

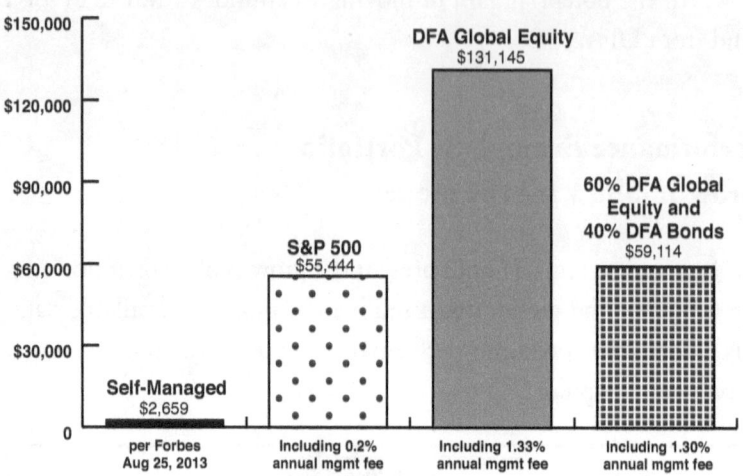

**Figure 5.2**
**Portfolio Comparison End Results**
*Past performance does not predict future performance*

Three points are particularly important concerning the above information.

1.  <u>Management Fees.</u> The DFA portfolios, as noted in Figure 5.2, are burdened with an annual management fee of 1.3 percent, vs. 0.2 percent for the S&P 500. This is because one can self-manage an S&P 500 index fund to get a total cost of 0.2 percent per year, whereas one must go through a financial advisor (or 401[k] or be an institution) to get a DFA product. Because the typical advisory fee for balances under $1 million is 1.00 percent per year, adding it to the 0.3 percent per year assumed average fee for DFA yields a total fee of 1.3 percent per year, the figure used in the graphics.

    However, even with the significantly higher fees, both the DFA Global Equity and Global 60/40 outperform the S&P

500, a benchmark that outperforms the overwhelming majority of similar-risk mutual funds over a long time span.

2. <u>Risk.</u> The DFA Global Equity Fund has a risk that's approximately equal to that of the S&P 500. Although DFA Global Equity has a slightly higher standard deviation than the S&P 500, one can argue that the Global Equity is lower risk than the S&P 500 because it's more diversified. But on the other side, one could argue that the Global Equity Fund is riskier than the S&P 500 not only because of its higher volatility, but also because of its international exposure.

   Again, as previously stated, standard deviation/volatility is not a perfect measure of risk. Keep in mind the DFA Global Equity Fund is comparable to the S&P 500 regarding risk and volatility, and the DFA Global Equity significantly outperforms the S&P 500, a very strong benchmark, even with a 1.00-percent advisory fee added to the Global Equity Fund but not the S&P 500.

   A lower risk investment, the DFA Global 60/40 Fund, has an annual standard deviation of approximately 10 percent, which is 40 percent less than that of the S&P 500. Hence, it's impressive that the DFA Global 60/40, with a 1.00-percent yearly financial advisory fee, still outperforms the S&P 500 without a financial advisory fee.

   However, one should note that all fixed income portfolios, including the bond side of the DFA 60/40, performed better during the mid-1970s through 2016 than can be expected going forward because of interest rates gradually sliding from the high teens in the late 1970s to near zero in 2016.

3. <u>Shape of the Lines.</u> Further to the point of risk, a simple visual analysis of the lines in Figure 5.1 reveals that the line of the DFA Global 60/40 portfolio is significantly smoother, or less jagged, than either the DFA Global Equity portfolio or the S&P 500. This is due to the DFA 60/40 providing a smoother, less-volatile ride because of its lower risk than either DFA Global Equity or the S&P 500.

## Example 2: A Professionally Managed DFA Portfolio vs. the DJIA from 2005–2018

While the first example is intriguing, you may ask, "How has an actual portfolio, managed per the strategies and tactics presented herein, performed versus the Dow Jones Industrial Average (DJIA) since, say, 2005?" (Schulz Financial started using DFA in 2004.) To fairly do this, one needs a portfolio that has had no cash inflows or outflows, other than management fees. Fortunately, I do have actual data to answer this question (Figure 5.3).

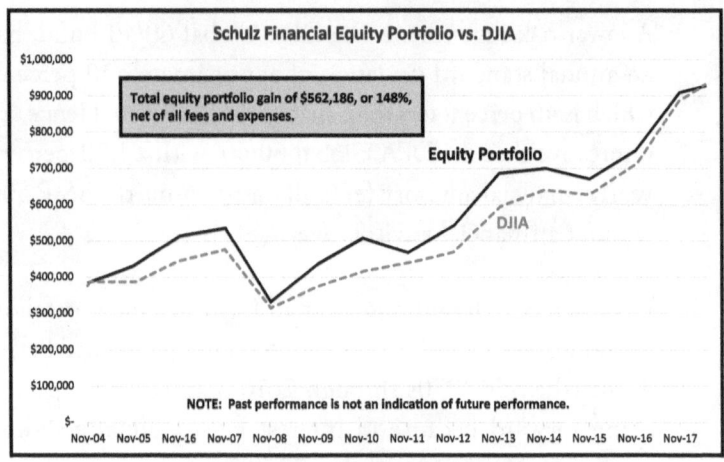

**Figure 5.3**
**A Professionally Managed DFA Equity Portfolio vs. the DJIA From November 2004 through August 2018**

As noted, the professionally managed DFA equity portfolio had total expenses of 1.3 percent per year, as compared with 0.2 percent per year for the DJIA.

In reviewing this information, keep in mind that 2008 was the worst calendar year for the stock market since the early 1930s. Also, international markets declined 45 percent or more in 2008, as compared with approximately 38 percent for domestic markets. This is relevant because nondomestic equities comprised more than 33 percent of the DFA portfolio. Hence, the DJIA had a stronger wind behind it than the DFA portfolio.

Furthermore, technology stocks, typically "growth" stocks, did unusually well compared with value stocks from 2014 to early 2018. Nevertheless, even with these disadvantages the hyper-diversified DFA portfolio had a geometric average return of 7.0 percent per year, net of all expenses (1.3 percent per year), and finished ahead of the self-managed DJIA with expenses of 0.2 percent per year.

Although the difference in August 2018 was small (0.7 percent), the DFA portfolio averaged an 8.6-percent lead over the subject time frame. Can someone accomplish such a performance without DFA? With the appropriate software and experience, an investment professional can come close to—although probably not equal—DFA's performance with non-DFA products.

You may rightfully ask: "Why hire a professional if I can do just about as well using the no-brainer DJIA?" This is a good and justifiable question.

**A Word on Financial Advisors.** The question on whether or not to hire a financial advisor is further justified if you personally have an analytical, unemotional and quantitative skill set and you can't find a financial advisor with a similar or superior skill set. Nevertheless, two heads are usually better than one, especially when you can leverage your assets 99 to 1, based on a 1-percent yearly management fee.

However, counterintuitively, analytical, experienced and appropriately educated financial advisors are few and far between.

_Rodney Schulz_

This is because one's personal financial situation is the second most private part of his or her life. Thus, unfortunately, most people make their investment decisions more on emotions than facts. These decisions especially include who to hire as a financial advisor. Hence, the financial advisory industry best rewards the advisors who can make the most emotionally driven appeal to prospective investors. Therefore, it is sad but true that most professional financial advisors are long on persuasion skills and short on quantitative skills. Further compounding this situation is the fact that most people with a good set of quantitative skills can make significantly more money working as something other than being a financial advisor.

Also, many financial advisors have a hundred or more clients. At this client load, it's unlikely the advisor knows every client well enough to understand and stay on top of that person's financial situation. But, if you can find a financial advisor with a strong set of analytical/quantitative skills who isn't overloaded, that kind of advisor can add significant value to your direction, confidence and net worth. A good financial advisor will provide value that goes beyond simply designing a portfolio.

Thus, when considering who to hire as a financial advisor, one must look at that person's skill set, experience, client load and ability to see the entire client value/net worth picture. This includes not only the client's investment portfolio, but also factors such as social security, pensions, risk tolerance, cash flow needs, home value and other financial factors.

## Example 3: A Moderate Risk Portfolio from 2006–2018

A similar example is from a Schulz Financial client portfolio that was 33 percent in bonds and 67 percent in equities. In summary, the portfolio grew 92 percent, by $786,000, from $852,000 to $1,640,000, net of all fees and expenses, over 12 years from mid-2006 to mid-2018. This equates to an arithmetic average growth rate of 7.7 percent per year, or a geometric average growth rate of 5.6 percent per year.

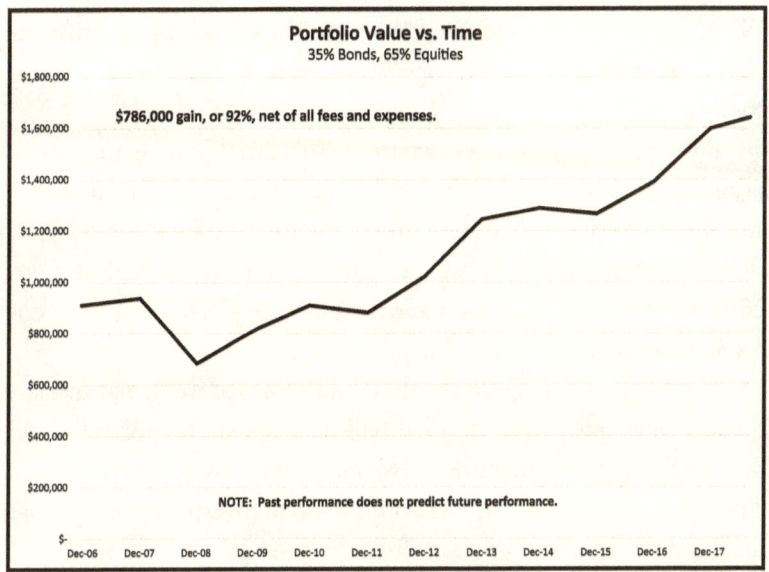

**Figure 5.4**
**A Professionally Managed DFA Portfolio**
**With 33% Bonds, 67% Equities**
Mid-2006 through Mid-2018

Keep in mind that the subject time horizon started just two years before the financial crisis of 2008. Thus, it was not a particularly good period for equity investments. Nevertheless, the client followed the advisor's recommendations, stayed with the game plan and was rewarded well for it.

## Example 4: A Retiree with an Aggressive Payout

Of course, many, if not most, investors are saving for retirement with the plan to ultimately live off their portfolio. This generates the question, "How well will the investment principles described herein hold up under difficult market conditions while still providing retirement income?" And, "How much income can one harvest from a portfolio while enduring these difficult conditions?" Additionally, "What happens when one is taking, as required by law, a significant distribution at and beyond age 70½, even with difficult market conditions?"

Fortunately, we have data from an actual retiree in such a situation. The retiree was beyond 70½ for the entire time frame and thus followed the required minimum distributions (RMDs) per IRS guidelines. And because the market was often in decline from 2004–2016, the average annual distribution equated to 6.3 percent per year of the initial portfolio value.

A 6.3 percent average annual distribution is of particular interest because any finance professional will declare that no portfolio will hold up to a 6.3-percent annual distribution over an extended period. This would be particularly challenging for an investment period that included the financial crisis of 2008.

Nevertheless, even with the investor withdrawing 75 percent of the initial portfolio value from February 2004 through March 2016, the portfolio retained 80 percent of its initial value (Figure 5.5). Specifically, the client started with a balance of $262,575, withdrew an average of $16,454 per year for 12 years for a total distribution of $197,452, and expired with a portfolio balance of $211,079. That's impressive!

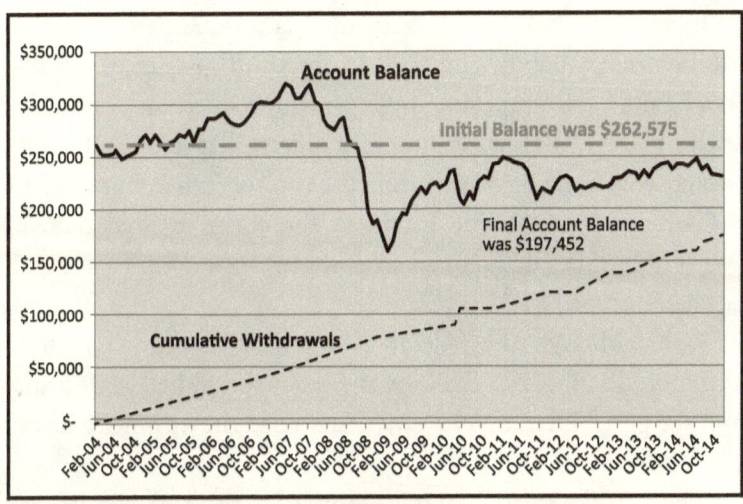

**Figure 5.5**
**Retiree Portfolio with an Average Annual 6.3% Distribution**
*Past performance does not predict future performance*

Although I would never recommend an average withdrawal rate of 6.3 percent per year, it will behoove you to research expected portfolio performance with elevated withdrawal rates. Why? Doing this will provide a "stress test" for a proposed portfolio while also forcing an advisor to get into territory no one wants to imagine but that reality may dictate, as it did in this case.

Also, withdrawing more than 4.5 percent per year is a dose of reality. Why? In this case, the retiree's RMD at age 87 was 7.9 percent of the portfolio's value on the preceding December 31st. And because of the retiree's life situation, none of the distribution money was reinvested into his portfolio.

The next logical question is: "What was in the subject retiree's portfolio?" Because the retiree had other secure fixed income sources (a corporate pension and social security), we started with 80 percent equities and 20 percent bonds. The first couple of years it was in index funds, after which we rolled it over to mutual funds from DFA.

In approximately 2011, we scaled it back to 60 percent equities and 40 percent bonds, and then in the third quarter of 2014 we reduced the equity exposure to 45 percent (55 percent bonds). If it weren't for the financial crisis and market collapse of 2008–2009 I would have rolled it back to the 60/40 mix earlier, but once the market started to decline I advised the client to hold onto his positions until the market had significantly recovered. Fortunately, the client listened.

Also, although the federal government suspended required minimum distributions in 2009, the client still pulled significantly from the portfolio in 2009. Why? He needed the income to sustain his lifestyle.

The key take-away from this example is that portfolios designed and patiently managed with the strategies and tactics described herein are robust and resilient.

## Summary Thoughts on the Performance Examples

As indicated by the charts and discussion, applying the concepts, strategies and tactics discussed in Chapters 1–4 yields strong investment returns per unit of risk and unit of cost. Further, portfolios designed and managed as discussed are robust and resilient. One does need to use common sense, as well as analytical expertise, when applying the information discussed in Chapters 1–4. However, overall, the methods produced yield performance not found with typical investment strategies.

Of course, as illustrated, one's return does depend on the portfolio's aggressiveness and time frame. Nevertheless, the time frame for Examples 2 through 4 were not a particularly good time for investing by historical standards. Some periods have been worse, such as the 1930s, but, overall, the period of 2004 to mid-2018 was not especially strong. For example, the DFA Global Equity strategy delivered an expense-included (1.3 percent per year) geometric average return of 8.7 percent for 2004–2017, compared with 11.9 percent for 1973–2017. That's a significant difference.

Another aspect to remember is the above portfolios, other than the S&P 500, were globally diversified. More specifically, the international component of each portfolio was 20 percent to 30 percent of the equity position.

Why is this important? It's a key point because international developed markets[5] delivered an expense-adjusted (1.3 percent per year) annual net return of 4.9 percent from 2004–2017, compared with 7.4 percent for the S&P 500. Thus, international developed markets significantly underperformed the U.S. markets for the subject time frame.

With this in mind, should one avoid non-U.S.A. markets? No, because ignoring them would be ignoring a significant piece of the global market, and at some point one can expect non-U.S.A. markets to improve. Also, because we live in a global economy, it's good to have a portfolio that has a global exposure.

---

1. www.pages.stern.nyu.edu., spring 2018 (since changed)
2. www.seekingalpha.com., spring 2018 (since changed)
3. *Forbes,* August 25, 2013.
4. Dimensional Fund Advisors 2014 Matrix Book (Global Equity and Global 60/40).
5. Morgan Stanley Composite Index for Europe, Asia and the Far East (MSCI EAFE), as reported by MSCI.

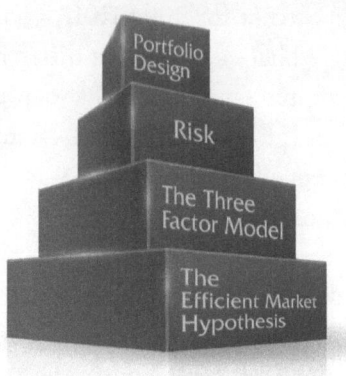

## CHAPTER 6

# A Closing Summary

By making it to this point you're a savvier investor than you were at the beginning of the book. Per the journey, the base of our investment pyramid is the efficient market hypothesis. And although this phrase may sound a bit academic, it describes a pragmatic concept that applies to everything from a bottle of ketchup at the supermarket to the value of your home and, yes, the value of the securities in your investment portfolio.

In short, the efficient market hypothesis states:

1) Free and open markets incorporate all information almost instantaneously.
2) Security price movements in a free and open market follow a random-walk model.

So rather than fretting about how to outsmart the market, you're ahead of the game if you let the market do the work for you. And fortunately, to your benefit, this will give you the highest return per unit of risk and cost.

More specifically, applying the efficient market hypothesis by using index funds or market-based funds can reduce your investment costs by 50 percent to 80 percent while improving your return and reducing your risk. That's exceptional!

While Chapter 1 presented the efficient market hypothesis, Chapter 2 presented the three-factor model. This model *explains* (remember, it doesn't predict—as no one is clairvoyant—but it explains) approximately 90 percent of a portfolio's return. The three factors are:

1) Stocks vs. bonds
2) Value vs. growth
3) Small vs. large

This is somewhat counterintuitive, as most investors and financial advisors focus on the industry, mutual fund company, portfolio manager and other factors that have signicantly less impact than the three factors listed above. This wastes both time and money.

By applying the three-factor model, combined with the efficient market hypothesis, you can disregard most of the financial headlines in today's news, as they're what you can now refer to as "investment pornography." Thus, from what is covered in Chapters 1 and 2, with your new knowledge and confidence, you can quit wasting time on things that don't matter.

Following the efficient market hypothesis and the three-factor model, we embarked on the oft-neglected issue of risk and uncertainty. As discussed, risk and return are connected. To get more return, you need to take on more risk. However, the key is to get as much return possible per unit of risk and unit of cost.

The unit of risk we established and discussed is the standard deviation of a portfolio. To sum it up, while security returns follow a random-walk model, a portfolio's standard deviation can be calculated with the appropriate software. Then, with the standard deviation determined, one can easily calculate a portfolio's 95-percent certainty range for a given span of time, as this certainty range is just the average return plus and minus two standard deviations.

For example, because the expected annual return of the S&P 500 is approximately 10 percent and its standard deviation is 17 percent, the 95-percent certainty range for an S&P 500 portfolio in one year is:

$$\text{Expected Value} = (1.10 \times \text{Today's Value})$$
$$+/- (34\% \text{ of Today's Value})$$

Thus, equity securities are volatile. However, as the length of time increases, the likelihood of ending up ahead of the starting point increases. Why? Because the market growth eventually outpaces its standard deviation.

Historically, if your time frame is one year, you have a one-out-of-three chance with an S&P 500 portfolio of ending up behind where you started. However, for a five-year period, that same portfolio has a nine-out-of-10 chance of ending up ahead. Therefore, if you're going to invest in equities, the longer your time frame, the better.

After quantifying risk and uncertainty, we moved to the subject of portfolio design. Using a simple food metaphor, we established that our portfolio ingredients and their proportions make a significant difference in portfolio performance. Further, based on Nobel Prize-winning work, we learned we can make a portfolio's risk/return characteristics greater than those of its individual components, just as the sum of the ingredients in a recipe, with the right things mixed in the right proportions and cooked for the right amount of time, result in a meal that tastes better than its individual ingredients.

In pulling this information together, we found that portfolios built using the strategies, methods and tactics of Chapters 1–4 yield superior returns to benchmarks such as the S&P 500 that commonly beat the overwhelming majority of portfolios. Additionally, after looking at multidecade hypothetical portfolios, we then looked at returns actually experienced by Schulz Financial clients from 2003 through mid-2018.

However, perhaps the best benefit of the strategies and tactics discussed is peace of mind. This comes from not second-guessing yourself and wasting time on the so-called "pundits" who are trying to justify their existence by reporting news that has already been factored into security prices. In addition to improving your peace of mind, you'll also have additional time for other, more enjoyable activities.

Thank you for your time, attention and consideration, as I wish you the best in your investing and financial future.

# A Word on Financial Advisors

## Some Troubling Facts

While one might think a financial advisor like myself would readily recommend hiring a financial advisor, the topic is really not that simple and merits an objective discussion, albeit a brief one.

Unfortunately, many financial advisors can barely add 3+2 when it comes to quantitative skills. Why is it that many, if not most, American financial advisors have poor numerical and analytical skills? The answer is multifold.

First, one's financial matters are the second most private part of their life. Hence, gaining access to one's personal financial matters, the first requirement of a financial advisor, often goes to those with the best psychological skills rather than the best analytical and numerical skills. Thus, while investment management is mostly a matter of logic, statistics and analysis, the advisors who make the most money are often those with the best sales skills, as opposed to numerical abilities.

Research has shown that people make decisions based on emotion and then look for the facts to justify what they've decided. Therefore, given how personal one's finances are to most people, investors will commonly choose an advisor who is adept at catering to their opinions and emotions, regardless of his or her numerical/quantitative/analytical skills. Naturally, this often leads to disastrous, or at least sub-par, results for the investor.

Compounding the situation is the fact that most people don't discuss how much money they personally lost through their chosen financial advisor. The reason is twofold—they don't want to reveal their personal finances, and they don't want others to know that they made a poor decision.

The next big problem underlying the financial advice arena is that only ~10 percent of those who set out to become financial advisors succeed in making a long-term living at it. This may be because the qualifications aren't high enough to screen out some individuals with limited capabilities. One does not even need to be a high school graduate to become a "financial advisor." In fact, one can earn a 100 score on the Securities and Exchange Commission's six-hour Series 7 securities license test with math skills that are not beyond high school algebra.

I understand this well, as I scored a 90 on the Series 7 exam when the national average was 73. The Series 7 is not an easy test, but it's mostly about recognizing the game of tricksmanship the government is trying to play instead of a straightforward, but demanding numerical and analytical test with relevant questions.

How can this happen? It's simple. The securities industry has a strong lobby and it recognizes that psychological skills trump analytical skills for bringing in business. Therefore, the industry does not want a test that will stop the good salesman who may not be very strong in math.

Another reason that only ~10 percent make it in a professional livelihood as a financial advisor is that remuneration is often 100 percent commission. You have to be willing to hear a whole lot of "no's" before hearing a "yes." For many people with good numerical and analytical skills, there are easier ways to make a good living than enduring years of rejections while building a clientele.

## Other Things to Consider

Most people who have built a portfolio in the hundreds of thousands or millions of dollars have better quantitative and analytical skills than many, if not most, professional financial advisors. Hence, they have little to gain by opening the second most private part of their life to the typical financial advisor.

However, because two good heads are usually better than one, a client does have something significant to gain by hiring a financial advisor with strong quantitative/analytical skills for several reasons.

First, even the most fact-based decision makers are prone to bias. Having a trusted advisor with good quantitative and analytical skills can help with hard-earned assets. It's more a matter of working through a problem together than simply following someone's advice. By working through things together, a smart client with a good advisor can find the optimal products, strategies and tactics to fit their situation.

Second, the advisor should be constantly benchmarking the client portfolio against other portfolios and metrics. Every quarter, through the way I bill, I evaluate each portfolio I manage against every other portfolio, as well as common metrics, such as the DJIA. I also apply some not-so-common metrics, such as those of emerging-market performance. Hence, I have a bird's-eye view of many portfolios, as opposed to the self-managed investor with only a single portfolio and a few well-published benchmarks.

Third, if one follows the recommendations of this book concerning low-cost index funds, ETFs and market-based products such as those offered by DFA, hiring an advisor is a low-cost proposition. Of course, one may immediately ask: "Why give away one percent a year, no matter how the portfolio performs, when I only have a long-term expected growth rate of, say, 8 percent?"

Looking at one's portfolio as a business puts things in perspective. If one pays $1/8^{th}$ for the financial advisor and another $1/30^{th}$ for the mutual fund, the profit remaining is $1.00 - 1/8^{th} - 1/30^{th}$, or 85 percent. How many businesses have an 85-percent profit margin? Not many. A long-term relationship with a competent financial advisor will generate good decisions and substantially decrease the chance of hitting a life-changing financial pothole.

Fourth, for married investors, a quantitative, analytical financial advisor is a good decision for the spouse if the more analytical of the two individuals dies first. It is good for the less analytical and investment-minded spouse to have a good advisor already in place.

How can one verify good numerical and quantitative skills? Methods can vary, but one should first look for a quantitatively based undergraduate degree (engineering, mathematics or accounting and not simply "business" or marketing). If one doesn't have a quantitatively based undergraduate degree, don't give them the opportunity to be your financial advisor.

Also, in addition to looking for the quantitative undergraduate degree, I recommend looking for multiple years of experience doing quantitative work. Spending multiple years in a quantitatively based professional job, not as a salesperson but as a number-cruncher, builds on good quantitative skills.

Don't be fooled by designations such as "RIA" or "CFP" or even "MBA." Most of these designations, by themselves, tell you very little. Additionally, don't simply look for someone "you can trust." A quantitative fool who means well may be the most trustworthy person in the world. However, investing is primarily a game of numbers and statistics. Thus, keep your standards high when it comes to your hard-earned money. Keep looking until you find the right set of skills that are possessed by someone with whom you can work.

What about the financial advisors who say "we have our number crunchers who will design your portfolio...." Avoid this type of advisor at all costs. Why? First, they are nothing but overhead that adds expense without adding value. And second, their emotional skill may lead you toward poor decisions.

If one has both the quantitative education and number-crunching experience, as well as being trustworthy, they may have the necessary starting skills to manage your life savings. Don't let your emotions drive the decision and simply decide on the person you like the most. Enabling you to be assured of meeting your future expenses is a financial/numerical challenge in addition to the personal qualities required; i.e., living within one's means. So when you seek a financial advisor, avoid turning your quest into a popularity contest.

# Thoughts on the U.S. Debt Situation
October 2018

## The Situation

Because the U.S. dollar is the world's reserve currency and because the U.S. stock markets represent 41 percent of the total world stock market capitalization[1], I would be remiss to write about investing today without commenting on the $22 trillion U.S. government debt.

What makes the $22 trillion national debt staggering is that U.S. federal tax receipts only total $3.4 trillion a year[2]. Therefore, the debt is approximately six times the annual federal revenue. Compounding the problem is the fact that the U.S. government spends $4.4 trillion per year, of which 0.4 trillion is interest on the federal debt with interest rates being near all-time lows.

While most people don't deal with numbers of this size (22 trillion is $22 \times 10^{12}$, or 22,000,000,000,000), the problem is simple. To get a quick understanding, just delete the last eight zeroes from the government debt total and the annual revenue and spending numbers, which leaves you with figures of $220,000, $34,000 and $44,000, respectively.

If you were a banker, would you loan a prospective homeowner $220,000 for a mortgage (with no down payment) when his annual income was $34,000 and his annual expenditures were $44,000? Of course not. The loan applicant would be sure to default on the $220,000 note.

What if the applicant were to cut cash expenditures by 23 percent so that his annual spending was only $34,000, of which $4,000 is for interest on debt? While such a cost reduction would be drastic, spending would still be 100% of income and leave the prospective lender in a precarious position.

Interest payments of $0.4 trillion on $22 trillion in debt equates to an average interest rate of 1.8 percent. This is compared with the 1926–2016 average U.S. Treasury Bill rate of 3.5 percent and U.S. Long-Term Government Bond rate of 5.7 percent. Clearly, because of market forces, interest rates at some point will increase, and when they do, it will squeeze a government and general population that are loath to face budgeting reality.

To be specific, if the average U.S. Government interest rate increased to the median of the historical average of the treasury bill and long-term government bonds, it would be 4.6 percent. Applying this figure to the $22 trillion national debt yields annual interest payments of approximately $1.0 trillion. Keep in mind the annual revenue is only $3.4 trillion.

The situation is not completely hopeless because the United States can overcome the situation through economic growth, which would increase tax revenue. The country could also pursue budget cuts to reduce the debt. However, to achieve that, the majority of American voters would need to base their votes on analysis and a sense of reality, instead of emotion, and the prospect of that is dubious at best. This opinion is based on the long history of Americans denying federal government budgeting reality, as reflected in their voting behavior.

This book is not about politics or public policy. However, one can easily see:

- The U.S. Government's financial situation is not sustainable.
- The problem is here and now, not decades into the future.
- The U.S. may be able to grow and cut its way out of the situation, but the likelihood of this happening is doubtful, thus leaving a significant chance for an eventual default.

A frequently asked question is: Why not just tax "the rich" or "the big corporations"? While this may attract many voters and politicians, the numbers don't bear out the solution. More specifically:

- Big Corporations. If the federal government *confiscated* 60 percent of the outstanding stock of publicly traded corporations (which, by the way, are largely owned by individuals, pension funds and endowment funds), the amount is just enough to pay off the national debt, with no money left over. And keep in mind, the federal government's annual expenditures would still be 129 percent of its annual revenues.
- Billionaires. If the U.S. federal government confiscated 100 percent of the assets of the billionaires in the United States, the amount would total approximately $2.7 trillion[3], or a mere 14 percent of the federal debt. Of course, if the federal government did start confiscating the assets, those owning the assets would soon figure out a way to get their assets out of the country or shield them from confiscation. Hence, the actual take would be something well under $2.7 trillion.

- <u>Taxing Everyone.</u> Generally, the states with the highest tax burdens tend to be the states that are having the most fiscal trouble. This argument quickly becomes politically charged, and this book is about personal finance, not politics. However, it's a basic human behavioral fact that money generally motivates people to work, and the more a government taxes, the lower the motivation of its populace to produce.

Although I'm not predicting a near-term financial collapse of the U.S. Government, governments have been defaulting on their debt or inflating their way out of it through currency devaluations, debt "restructuring" and other means for as long as governments have been borrowing money—a very long time.

## Thoughts for Investing

Because it is not unrealistic to envision the U.S. Government defaulting on its debt and/or other obligations, such as Social Security, a prudent investor would be wise to consider such a situation when evaluating his portfolio. However, the good news is that capitalism is globally marching forward. Technological advances, including the Internet, cell phones, television and increased mobility, have continued to accelerate the advance of capitalism, particularly over the past two decades.

With this in mind, consider the following:

- If the U.S. Government defaults on its debt, would you deny yourself your daily Diet Coke or Starbucks splurge?
- If the U.S. Government defaults on its debt, do you think the people in your state and Congressional district will throw their senator and U.S. representative out of office? Probably not.

- Conversely, would a corporation such as Coca-Cola, ExxonMobil, Apple or IBM terminate its chief executive officer if he leads the corporation into financially defaulting on its obligations? Absolutely. In fact, terminations at many levels would likely start long before the company's financials deteriorated to default status.
- Where does true value lie?
  o Paper with green numbers and faces printed on it? or,
  o Shares of viable corporations that create value for their customers and shareholders, no matter what the measure of the value?
- Clearly, the better, safer investment is a broadly diversified portfolio as outlined in this book. In other words, and counterintuitively, one can make a strong argument that a highly diversified corporate security portfolio has a lower risk of default than government bonds.

To be sure, the stock market will be volatile if the U.S. Government defaults on its debt and/or pursues inflationary monetary practices. Nevertheless, with or without the U.S. Government, capitalism will march forward.

To put it in simple terms, people, from any country, don't travel across the oceans in wooden ships any longer (except possibly for the refugees trying to escape highly socialistic economies). To the contrary, almost everyone goes to work every day to make his or her life better. This, in turn, drives capitalism and markets. Hence, while investing in stocks and bonds is not without volatility, investing in a well-diversified global portfolio, as outlined in this book, is probably as safe an investment as one can make.

1. www.worldbank.org; At the end of 2017, the total global stock market capitalization was $79 trillion, of which $32 trillion was in the U.S. stock market.

2. www.thebalance.com, citing the U.S. Office of Management and Budget for October 1, 2018.

3. Based on analysis of www.billionairemailinglist.com, updated in January 2018.

# ADDENDUM III

# Annuities

A client once asked me, "Can't I just give all of my money to some organization and get a guaranteed monthly stipend for the rest of my life?" My answer was yes, through either an immediate annuity or a charitable remainder trust, but each have three BIG caveats:

1) You lose some or all control of investment options and the way your money is invested.
2) The "guaranteed" stipend is only as guaranteed as the financial viability of the institution backing the product. What looks very stable and dependable now may look significantly different just a year or two from now, let alone in 10 or 20 years if you're still alive. For specific examples of short payouts, look at the retired public employees of Cedar Falls, Rhode Island, and the pensions of many retired steelworkers.

3) When you expire, some or all of your assets go to the company/institution that "guaranteed" the monthly stipend.

Investors ultimately realize this and are thus somewhat or strongly reluctant to hand over their money to an annuity. However, because annuities typically have a high commission for the sales representative, they're pushed hard by insurance and financial service companies.

Why are annuities high-commission products? Because the insurance company gets all or a big part of the asset, either immediately or at the end of your life. Do I offer annuities? No, because the way I recommend that investors manage their retirement nest egg is better than any annuity product I have seen to date.

However, many non-profit organizations, and particularly universities, offer a "planned giving" product called a "charitable remainder trust." Using this product one can make a donation to an organization and receive, in return, an income stream for life.

Further, depending on one's tax situation and location of residence, he may be able to deduct a significant percentage of the donation from his income tax, and a portion of the future stipends may be tax-free.

Therefore, when one compares the after-tax impact of a charitable remainder trust with that of an insurance company annuity, he may often find the charitable remainder trust option to be competitive with or possibly superior to an insurance company annuity.

Historically, I've evaluated planned giving quotes from The University of Kansas Endowment Association and Oklahoma State University's endowment organization. I found them to be highly competitive with insurance company products.

Generally, all of the universities and non-profits follow similar payout guidelines and use standard software to make the calculations. Hence, their payout amounts tend to be close to one another. However, the financial viability may vary significantly from one organization to the other, so do your homework and look into the underlying assets vs. the future liabilities of the organization. To the best of my knowledge, one can also create a self-managed charitable remainder trust.

With the aforementioned in mind, you may wish to ask the following questions:

Future Beneficiary. When you expire, would you prefer that your hard-earned money go to the insurance company, its shareholders and its employees, or to a non-profit organization or charity of your choice?

Trustworthiness. To be sure, all organizations have their shortcomings. But, which would you trust more, an insurance company or a charity/university endowment fund? Different individuals may give different answers, but public non-profit organizations tend to be more transparent than most companies.

Conservatism Factor. Although both options have to follow laws and guidelines as to how the assets are invested, which would you trust more to follow a conservative route that most strongly ensures your future income stream: the charity/university or the insurance company?

Additional Benefits. Universities and charities often have dinners and other functions. Although the organizations' objectives are always to raise more money from people like you, the dinners and other functions can be enjoyable and a great place to meet, socialize and network with other accomplished individuals. In comparison, you may wish to find someone who has purchased an immediate annuity from an insurance company and ask if her annuity salesperson has ever taken her and her husband to dinner.

Again, when choosing an organization to back a charitable remainder trust, one would be wise to look at the asset base, length of existence, mission, financial viability, hard assets, oversight and other factors before trusting them to provide a future income stream. With this in mind, I generally recommend universities and hospitals over other organizations.

To be sure, I'm not explicitly recommending insurance company annuities or charitable remainder trusts from non-profit and charitable organizations. Each investor has different skill sets and objectives, so each investor needs to choose the scenario that best fits him or her. However, I believe for most people the best investment option is to follow the strategies and tactics laid out in Chapters 1–4, most of which were developed by Nobel Prize winners or their peers.

## ADDENDUM IV

# Global Allocation

One question yet to be addressed is, "How much money should I invest in overseas markets vs. domestic markets?" Before we embark on this discussion, we need to consider the strategy within each country.

In short, the strategy for each country should follow the strategy outlined in this book for free and open markets (not controlled by the government). To summarize:

- The efficient market hypothesis (Chapter 1) holds within markets around the world.
- The three-factor model (Chapter 2) holds within markets around the world.
- Risk (Chapter 3) outside of the U.S.A. can be addressed with uncertainty, standard deviations, and bell curves. Again, uncertainty is not a perfect definition of risk, but it's a good place to start.

- Mean Variance Optimization (MVO, Chapter 4) is a mathematical calculation and thus holds for free and open markets around the world.

Now that we have addressed the strategy within each country/region, the next place to turn is how much to invest within each country/region.

## The Global Equity Balance

In summary, the global equity balance by region of the world is approximately:

- 43 percent U.S.A.[1]
- 19 percent Europe
- 33 percent Asia
- 5 percent other

Hence, if all countries were of equal risk and one had no investment biases (neither of which hold in reality), one could logically argue that an investor's allocation by region would equal the percentage share of each region in the global equity market. More specifically, in applying this model, if one were to invest $100,000, the allocation would be:

- $43,000 in the U.S.A. equity markets
- $19,000 in European equity markets
- $33,000 in Asian equity markets
- $5,000 in other equity markets

Also, the balance within each segment would be weighted accordingly. For example, if the German equity markets comprised 25 percent of the total European equity market, 25 percent of the $19,000 invested in Europe would go to the German markets. Then, the amount in each German company would be allocated per the strategy outlined in Chapters 1–4.

This may sound like an impossible algebra problem, but bear with me. The end result is both cheap and easy to execute.

Further complicating the issue is that all countries are not equal in risk, and no investor is unbiased regarding his country of domicile. Nevertheless, based on hundreds (if not thousands) of investment model runs I've personally executed—combined with the global equity balance and the risk/return profile of different countries—a good place for American investors to start is:

- 65 percent of the equity mix in U.S.A. markets.
- 27 percent of the equity mix in "developed" markets.
- 8 percent of the equity mix in "emerging" markets.

Why the switch in international regions from Europe, Asia and others to "developed" and "emerging" markets? For a variety of reasons beyond the scope of this book (we want to keep it simple) it's better to put countries like the Czech Republic, Brazil, South Africa and Thailand together within "emerging" markets and put Japan, Germany, Canada and Australia together within "developed" markets.

How much should one vary from the 65/27/8 model? It depends on one's risk tolerance and other personal factors. This may sound a bit nebulous, but keep in mind that capital, i.e., money, flows around the globe with minimal friction. Thus, when investing, it's always best to keep an eye on the global equity balance. Fortunately, because of market correlation, that balance seldom changes by much overnight. Hence, one can develop a personalized strategy and adjust in small increments as necessary along the way.

---

1. visualcapitalist.com, fall 2018 (since changed), with consideration of figures from the World Bank and other sources.

## ADDENDUM V

# A Suggested Financial Plan for Retirement

Every suggestion I've seen in publications such as the *Wall Street Journal* assumes a portfolio size at retirement of, say $1 million, a constant annual distribution of, for example, 4.5 percent of the initial $1 million, or $45,000 regardless of market conditions, and then applies an estimated lifespan. However, this approach has at least two significant flaws. First, market conditions change and returns are random. And second, we don't know how long we will live.

To be more realistic, I'm proposing the following:

1) First, alter the mindset to a distribution method that will likely last indefinitely if one follows the investment methods outlined in this book. This way you don't have to worry about outliving your portfolio.

2) Second, reduce the fixed annual distribution on a $1 million portfolio to 2.5 percent of that amount, or $25,000, taken in monthly or quarterly installments.
3) Third, have a floating quarterly distribution of 0.5 percent of the portfolio's value on the last day of the quarter. (This floating distribution equals 2.0 percent per year). Thus, if the portfolio has a value of $1 million at the end of each quarter, you will receive $5,000 per quarter, or $20,000 per year, in addition to the $25,000 per year mentioned above. This gives you a total annual distribution of $45,000, or 4.5 percent, on a balance of $1 million.
4) Fourth, invest approximately 60 percent of the portfolio in equities and 40 percent in short- to intermediate-term, investment grade nongovernment bonds. This will allow for one to pull from the fixed income assets when market downturns occur.
5) Fifth, do not retire until your dwelling is fully or mostly paid for, thus opening the opportunity of a maximum-value reverse mortgage if the market has a long, sustained decline starting immediately after retirement.

The key to this, in addition to the investment strategies and tactics outlined in this book, is having two-fifths, or 40 percent, of the periodic distribution amount float. This makes it less likely the portfolio will collapse.

Should the market have a sustained decline, one can substitute the reverse mortgage for part or all of the fixed distribution amount, depending on factors such as home value and the age of the investor. If having a constant level of ongoing income is important, you can fix a part of the income stream by using annuities or charitable remainder trusts. However, inflation can reduce the purchasing power of the fixed income stream. Also, you need to realize that to get the maximum utility from an asset that varies in value, such as an investment portfolio, you need to allow the distribution to vary to some degree with the market. This is the mathematical reality of the situation.

This isn't as bad as it may initially sound. For example, if equity markets decline 20 percent (the definition of a "bear market") from the initial value of $1 million, the annual distribution would change per the following:

First, assuming the portfolio is 60 percent equities and 40 percent bonds, and assuming the bond markets stay level during the equity market decline, the $1,000,000 million portfolio would decline by:

Portfolio Result: $400,000 + [(1 – 0.2) x $600,000] = $880,000

Initial Distribution: (.025 x 1,000,000) + (.02 x 1,000,000) = $45,000

to

Bear Market Distribution: (.025 x 880,000) + (.02 x 880,000) = $39,600

In other words, a market decline of 20 percent would reduce the distribution by only 12 percent. And to further reduce the long term impact of taking a distribution during a bear market one can take an outsize portion of the distribution (more than 40 percent) from the fixed income portion of the portfolio. Of course, a fixed income amount from Social Security, a pension plan, an annuity or a charitable remainder trust will further reduce the fluctuation percentage of the retiree's total annual income.

## A Word on Pensions and Other Forms
## of Fixed Retirement Income

One of the questions an investor constantly wrestles with is, "What amount of my portfolio should be fixed-income and what amount should be equity?" While the root of this question goes back to one's risk tolerance and time horizon, one could still ask, "How should I treat the pension or social security piece of my retirement?"

In short, because a pension has a fixed payout amount, the investor should treat it as a fixed income part of the portfolio. Further, based on annuity payout tables and a variety of factors, it's reasonable to estimate that the underlying fixed-income value is 1 divided by .05 times the annual payout amount. In other words, if one has a pension income stream of $10,000 per year it equates to a fixed income portfolio amount of $200,000 (1 divided by 0.05 times $10,000). Hence, if your social security checks total $25,000 per year, one should consider Social Security as having a fixed income value of $25,000 divided by 0.05, which equals $500,000.

This is significant in the case of allocating assets during retirement. For example, if one has a portfolio of $1 million plus $25,000 from a pension or social security, the total portfolio is really $1,500,000, with $500,000 of it representing an immovable amount in fixed income. Therefore, if one desires an equity-to-bond mix of 60/40, the equity percentage would be:

0.60 x $1,500,000 (not $1,000,000) = $900,000

and the bond investment would be:

$1,000,000 - $900,000 = $100,000

This leaves a total portfolio comprising:

$$\$900{,}000 + \$100{,}000 + \$500{,}000 \text{ (the underlying}$$
$$\text{value of the pension)} = \$1.5 \text{ million}$$

Again, the equity percentage is $900,000 divided by $1.5 million, or 60 percent. Similarly, the fixed income percentage is $600,000 ($100,000 + $500,000), or 40 percent of $1.5 million.

Would I recommend that a retiree in the above situation put 90 percent of his investment portfolio in equities? Definitely not, as I would recommend a lower percentage there and a higher percentage in bonds. Nevertheless, the above situation illustrates how easy it is to undervalue a pension and unwittingly overweight the fixed income portion of a retirement portfolio.

One uplifting conclusion from this discussion is that if you have a highly diversified, low-cost portfolio invested per the previous chapters, your Social Security/pension payment makes your overall portfolio more stable than what your emotions tell you by simply looking at your investment portfolio balance. In short, you need to look at all the assets and sources of income when calculating the investment portfolio allocation, particularly leading up to and during retirement. Nevertheless, keep in mind that governments and pensions have been defaulting on agreements/debt obligations as long as governments and pensions have existed, which is a very long time.

# ADDENDUM VI

# Selected Articles, Papers and Presentations

### Written by the Author
### As well as Expert Witness Experience

Having an undergraduate degree in petroleum engineering, Schulz has a long-running involvement in the Society of Petroleum Engineers (SPE), although his primary current focus is personal investment finance. While it is beyond the scope of this book to examine the many overlaps between oil and gas production economics and personal investment finance, one item of key importance is forecasting future cash flows.

A personal investment portfolio's future value has 1.5 degrees of uncertainty: one degree for market uncertainty and half a degree of uncertainty for future additions and withdrawals (only half a degree because a person has a significant degree of control over these items). In comparison, forecasting oil and gas production value is much more complex, having five degrees of significant uncertainty: future oil price, future gas price, (both oil and gas prices are far more volatile than most equity buckets such as the S&P 500) reservoir parameters, production hardware & well stimulation uncertainties and operating cost (which can be highly variable for oil and gas production assets). Thus, by mastering future oil and gas production value to the point that he is internationally sought after to teach on the subject, Schulz is far more qualified than most financial advisors in his ability to forecast future personal investment portfolios.

Another key overlap between the professions is the random walk of both security prices as well as oil and gas prices. Additional benefits for Rod, and you, the reader, include the experience of teaching one on twenty when many of those in the audience are both highly analytical and skeptical, as well as the real exposure to international business.

Professionals, managers and executives that Rod has taught have come from Shell, Chevron, ConocoPhillips, the California joint venture between ExxonMobil and Shell, Occidental, BHP Billiton, Saudi Aramco, Abu Dhabi National Oil Company (ADNOC), Pemex (the national oil company of Mexico), the international management consulting firm of McKinsey & Company, the globally recognized reservoir engineering firms of Ryder Scott and Netherland Sewell, academics, consultants and many small to mid-size independent oil and gas companies.

NOTE: The Journal of Petroleum Technology (*JPT*) is the flagship publication of the Society of Petroleum Engineers (SPE), an organization founded in 1957 from a predecessor organization that goes back to 1871. SPE now has 180,000 members in 143 countries.

## Published Articles:

"Oil and Efficient Market Theory," *JPT*, March 2007, pages 20–22.

"Three Steps to a Risked Revenue Forecast," *JPT*, July 2011, pages 74–76.

"Common Sense Economics for Projects," *JPT*, October 2009, pages 31–33.

"The Reason to Expect Prolonged USD 30–60 Oil," *JPT*, October 2016.

"Mulling Metrics," *Oil and Gas Investor*, August 2012, pages 77–79.

## Published and Copyrighted Papers:

"Risk, Reward, Metrics and Volatility," SPE paper 130104, presented at the SPE biannual Hydrocarbon Economics Evaluation Symposium, Dallas, TX, March 8–9, 2010.

"An Unconventional but Definitive Analysis of a Field's Production Improvement," SPE paper 117433, presented at the SPE/AAPG Joint Eastern Regional Meeting, Pittsburgh, PA, October 11–15, 2008.

Two of Schulz's papers have been used in the petroleum engineering curriculum at The University of Kansas.

## Selected Presentations:

Instructor, "Oil & Gas Economics and Uncertainty," a one day seminar (initially a two day seminar) developed by Schulz, at the following conferences as well as a number of stand-alone events:

- 2019 Abu Dhabi International Petroleum Exhibition and Conference (ADIPEC)
  - o 150,000 attendees from 139 countries
  - o Taught at the headquarters hotel of the Abu Dhabi National Oil Company (ADNOC).
  - o The United Arab Emirates, of which ADNOC is the primary producer, is the eight largest oil producing country in the world.
  - o Conference speakers included former U.S. Secretary of State Condaleeza Rice and the Secretary General of the Organization of Petroleum Exporting Countries (OPEC), as well as many other global level dignitaries and countless executives.
- 2019 SPE Annual Conference and Exhibition (ATCE) in Calgary, Canada
  - o ATCE is SPE's flagship annual technical conference.
- 2017 Mexican National Petroleum Congress
  - o Mexico is the tenth largest oil producing country in the world and the Mexican National Petroleum Congress is the country's flagship annual oil and gas production event.
- 2015 SPE Annual Technology Conference and Exhibition
- 2013 SPE biannual Hydrocarbon Economics Evaluation Symposium
- 2011 SPE Western Regional Meeting

Speaker at many other conferences and meetings as well as a guest lecturer at The University of Kansas for its drilling engineering class.

## Selected Expert Witness Experience:

- Expert to the Examiner appointed by the United States Bankruptcy Court in Corpus Christi, Texas to determine the value of the oil and gas assets involved with a $30+ million bankruptcy case.
- Expert witness recruited by the international law firm of Fulbright & Jaworski for their client in a $30 million (determined by Schulz) case against Chesapeake Energy regarding Haynesville Shale assets.
  - o Chesapeake, at the time, was one of the five largest natural gas producers in the United States.
  - o Both Fulbright and Jaworski are key attorneys in history. Leon Jaworski was the attorney who prosecuted Richard Nixon for the Watergate scandal, and R.C. Fulbright was instrumental in founding the Texas Medical Center, now the largest medical center in the world.